DATE DUE

MESSAGE EFFECTS RESEARCH

THE GUILFORD COMMUNICATION SERIES

Editors
Theodore L. Glasser
Department of Communication, Stanford University

Howard E. Sypher
Department of Communication Studies, University of Kansas

Advisory Board

Charles Berger	Peter Monge	Michael Schudson
James Carey	Barbara O'Keefe	Ellen Wartella

MESSAGE EFFECTS RESEARCH: PRINCIPLES OF DESIGN AND ANALYSIS
Sally Jackson

CRITICAL PERSPECTIVES ON MEDIA AND SOCIETY
Robert K. Avery and David Eason, *Editors*

THE JOURNALISM OF OUTRAGE: INVESTIGATIVE REPORTING AND AGENDA BUILDING IN AMERICA
David L. Protess, Fay Lomax Cook, Jack C. Doppelt, James S. Ettema, Margaret T. Gordon, Donna R. Leff, and Peter Miller

MASS MEDIA AND POLITICAL TRANSITION: THE HONG KONG PRESS IN CHINA'S ORBIT
Joseph Man Chan and Chin-Chuan Lee

STUDYING INTERPERSONAL INTERACTION
Barbara M. Montgomery and Steve Duck, *Editors*

VOICES OF CHINA: THE INTERPLAY OF POLITICS AND JOURNALISM
Chin-Chuan Lee, *Editor*

COMMUNICATION AND CONTROL: NETWORKS AND THE NEW ECONOMIES OF COMMUNICATION
G. J. Mulgan

CASE STUDIES IN ORGANIZATIONAL COMMUNICATION
Beverly Davenport Sypher, *Editor*

Message

Effects

Research

*Principles of Design
and Analysis*

SALLY JACKSON

THE GUILFORD PRESS
New York   London

To Keith and Gerry Jackson

© 1992 The Guilford Press
A Division of Guilford Publications, Inc.
72 Spring Street, New York, NY 10012

Printed in the United States of America

This book is printed on acid-free paper.

Last digit is print number: 9 8 7 6 5 4 3 2 1

Library of Congress Cataloging-in-Publication Data

Jackson, Sally Ann, 1952–
    Message effects research: principles of design and
analysis / Sally Jackson.
        p. cm. — (The Guilford communications series)
    Includes bibliographical references and index.
    ISBN 0-89862-316-2
    1. Communication—Research—Methodology. 2.
Communication— Philosophy. I. Title. II. Series.
P91.3.J3   1992
302.2'072—dc20   92-11714
                                                    CIP

PREFACE

This book is about how to design experiments to find out about message effects. The design problems peculiar to this area of study came to my attention as I was reviewing a manuscript submitted for publication in a communication research journal. My task as a reviewer was to evaluate the quality of the manuscript, to make recommendations to the journal editor on whether or not to publish it, and to make suggestions for improvement of the manuscript if possible. There are many ways to approach this task. Mine is to read any theoretical essay or empirical report as an argument for a claim and to search for any counterargument that might be raised against the claim. The manuscript I was reviewing put forward several interesting claims about the effects of message features on responses to messages. The data presented in the paper were treated as evidence for the claims, but inspection of the details of the data convinced me that the evidence was an insufficient basis for the claims. The data could as easily have been used to argue a rival hypothesis as to argue the claim itself.

There is nothing remarkable in this; reviewers often notice rival hypotheses, and most often the source of the difficulty is some error in procedure or some oversight on the part of the experimenter.

In this particular case, the source of the difficulty was not what would normally be called an error or oversight—at least not on the part of the experimenter. The experiment was designed in a fashion almost indistinguishable from other experiments on message effects, and it employed every known safeguard against invalidity. There was in the experiment a very minor deviation from the standard experimental design: the use of two instantiations of the message treatment contrast instead of one. This minor deviation did not make the experiment less valid than other such experiments. It did call attention to a source of invalidity that had been present in many other studies of standard design, but unnoticed. The deviant design revealed the problem that the standard design concealed.

I pointed out the problem in my comments to the editor and the author of the experiment, and lengthy correspondence followed. Meanwhile, I began an independent exploration of the problem, searching the previously published message effects literature for other examples of it. What I found was that the vast majority of such experiments used single instantiations of their treatment variables, a design decision that on the one hand made the experiments vulnerable to certain identifiable threats to validity and on the other hand concealed that vulnerability.

The problem, once noticed, seemed easily correctable, so Scott Jacobs and I wrote a paper describing the problem and making some general suggestions for how to avoid it in design of experiments. This paper gave rise to a large number of critical replies, keeping me and my colleagues busy for some years dealing with the many objections and challenges to the proposal. In some cases, the challenges pointed to the need for justification of the proposal, and in other cases to the need for development of research strategies. My colleagues and I have attempted to respond to all of the reasonable challenges, but many of these are such that only research practice can lead to any real solution.

This is the way methodology advances. People notice that something can go wrong or has gone wrong in the routine ways of generating evidence for empirical claims. Then they find ways of correcting for whatever it is that can go wrong. Perhaps other people find ways the corrections can go wrong. This book is a progress report on a search for a set of solutions.

The book summarizes and extends work initiated in collaboration with a number of people. The final responsibility for this book is mine, but it would never have been possible without the contributions of Scott Jacobs, Daniel J. O'Keefe, and Dale E. Brashers, my continuing partners in the development of these ideas. My indebtedness to these colleagues will be clear throughout the text, and I owe them each additional appreciation for reading and commenting on the manuscript.

Many other colleagues have contributed in one way or another to the development of my thinking about these issues. Dale Brashers and Joseph Massey helped me to develop some of the material presented in Chapter 5. I have benefited from the insights and/or encouragement of a number of other scholars with whom I have discussed ideas related to this project, especially Michael Burgoon, Jesse G. Delia, Dale Hample, Barbara J. O'Keefe, Robert D. McPhee, and Charles A. Willard. More general intellectual debts are owed to Ruth Anne Clark and Joseph W. Wenzel, the former for shaping my views of method and the latter for shaping my views of argument. I also owe thanks to Peter Wissoker and Howard Sypher for their patience and encouragement. Finally, to my husband Scott Jacobs and our son Curtis Jackson-Jacobs, thanks are due for the many sacrifices that must be made when any family member is engaged in a project of this kind.

This book was written during my year as a Fellow of the Netherlands Institute for Advanced Study in the Humanities and Social Sciences, 1989–1990, and would not otherwise have been possible. NIAS provided not only the time needed for the writing, but the conditions needed for the thinking. Partial support for the project was also provided by the University of Oklahoma Office of the Provost. Preliminary work related to the book was supported by a grant from the Central States Speech Association, in the form of the Federation Prize Award for 1983.

CONTENTS

ONE

Empirical Claims about Message Effects

Central to the study of communication is the message. Research in communication may focus on any sort of message: unplanned utterances such as remarks made in conversation, formal prepared discourses such as speeches and essays, repeatable texts such as product advertisements, or anything else that one person says, writes, or presents to another. Messages are the most distinctive and characteristic object of study for communication research.

Much of communication research is aimed at developing general claims about the properties or effects of messages. This observation, which I take to be relatively noncontroversial, suggests that communication research methodology should be especially attentive to any problems involved in making claims about messages, and that communication research might profit from giving sustained critical attention to the nature of messages. All fields of study require specialized methodology tailored to their objects of study; communication research is no exception. For communication research, this specialized methodology must be tailored to messages and message users.

This book considers one issue that must be confronted by communication research methodology: the problem of evaluating and documenting message *effects*. By message effects, I mean variations in communication outcomes that follow from choices made about the design or presentation of a message. To ask whether one type of message is more effective than another in meeting a specified objective is to ask about the effect of message type. Questions of just this sort arise in many superficially different lines of research, but especially in the context of social influence research and interpersonal communication research, where the characteristic task is to identify strategic variables that can be linked to communication processes or communication outcomes.

In virtually every area of communication research, there are an indefinitely large number of unanswered questions about message effects. We would like to know, for example, whether persuasive appeals based on the audience's self-interest are more or less effective than persuasive appeals based on altruism. We would like to know whether people can tell the difference between strong and weak arguments. We would like to know how self-disclosure contributes to relationship development. We would like to know whether political debates affect voting intentions. We would like to know whether commercial advertisements are more or less persuasive when they mention the names of competing products. The task of the communication researcher interested in such questions is to propose answers and to offer grounds for believing the answers to be correct.

Now, the methodological problems involved in finding out anything worth knowing about message effects are extremely difficult and subtle. The approach taken in this book is that our efforts to overcome these problems depend on a continuing process of critical dialogue. While trying to find out things about message effects, we must simultaneously try to find out things *about the process of finding out*. In trying, for example, to find out whether self-interest is more or less effective than altruism as a basis for persuasion, we will have to confront the problem of how to represent abstract categories of appeals (like self-interest and altruism), and we will have to consider whether the advantage of one appeal type over another is consistent enough from case to case to make any sort of generalization meaningful. When we defend a general claim about message effects or critically examine the evidence offered for such a claim, we stand to gain not only some substantive increase in our knowledge about messages, but also an improvement in our ability to generate additional substantive knowledge. Much of the time, the grounds we give for believing that messages of a certain kind have a certain effect will be inadequate in some obvious way. Our methods for researching message effects can advance only as we learn to identify these inadequacies and avoid them.

A useful metaphor will be to think of the research process argumentatively, as a process of arguing for and against empirical claims.

We progress in our knowledge of message effects by putting forward strong arguments in favor of new principles, and we progress in our methodology by coming to better understandings of how to make strong arguments.

MAKING A CASE FOR A CAUSAL CLAIM

To understand the research-as-argumentative metaphor, consider what is involved in the demonstration of a causal relationship. Essentially, the research community's task can be seen as one of deciding whether or not to accept a causal claim, of the form X *causes* Y. Research contributes to such a decision by generating evidence in favor of or in opposition to it. Evidence in favor of a claim like X *causes* Y must include documentation of covariation between an acceptable operationalization of X and an acceptable operationalization of Y; it may also include reasons to believe that the covariation cannot be explained other than as influence of X on Y. Evidence against such a claim might include substantiated challenges to the genuineness of the apparent covariation (charges, for example, of measurement invalidity or artifact) or competing explanations of the covariation (claims that Y *causes* X or that Z *causes* Y, *and* X's *association is incidental*). The two central issues involved in either supporting or opposing a causal claim, which we will refer to as "the question of covariation" and "the question of cause," define the sort of case that must be presented if a causal claim is to be taken seriously.

The paradigmatic form for defense of a causal claim is the controlled experiment. It is not, of course, the only possible form, nor is it a form guaranteed to produce a strong argument. It is paradigmatic in the sense of being tailored to the two central issues involved in defending a causal claim. An experiment involves observation (of an outcome) under contrasting conditions. The contrast between the conditions, to be relevant, must involve differing "values" of the causal variable. The cause must be present in one condition and absent in the other, or present in differing degrees across conditions. Assuming a difference in outcome under the contrasting conditions, a causal claim can be defended to the extent that it is possible to preclude other explanations of the difference in outcome.

Experiments have a well-known advantage over other ways of assessing covariation. Obviously, it would be possible to document covariation between X and Y by locating events in which the values of X vary naturally, and to observe the association of Y with X in these events. But covariation between naturally occurring values of

X and Y is not ordinarily a very convincing basis for the claim that X *causes* Y, because $X–Y$ covariation is equally consistent with three contradictory sorts of claims: that X *causes* Y, that Y *causes* X, and that *Z causes Y, and X's association is incidental*. An experiment precludes *Y causes* X by directly controlling the value of X, independently of the value of Y, and it limits the plausibility of *Z causes Y* to the extent that it succeeds in "holding constant" across observational conditions all variables other than X that might be suspected of affecting Y.

So far, we have been talking in a very abstract way about causal claims and the lines of argument required to support them in general. Situated within an actual empirical context, the task of building an adequate defense of a causal claim will change shape depending on substantive knowledge about what sorts of influences are possible, and substantive beliefs about what is problematic in observation. Within the social sciences, a very fundamental substantive constraint on empirical arguments is the fact of human individuality. The social scientist experimenting on people always faces the problem of separating effects of a causal variable on response from variations in response that reflect only the individual characteristics of the respondent. When the effect of a treatment is evaluated by comparing responses of people given the treatment with responses of people not given the treatment, the contrasted observational conditions differ in two ways, not one: first, in the presence or absence of the treatment, and second, in the individual and particular people who were observed under each condition.

The problem of how to separate the treatment's influence on human response from the sheer individual variability of response is the paradigmatic methodological problem of the experimental social sciences. Routine solutions to this problem have been well worked out. These solutions depend on the use of many respondents for each experimental treatment, random assignment of respondents to treatments (when subjects cannot be given all treatments), and statistical separation of treatment effects from individual effects. Notice that these solutions do not in fact result in the isolation of the treatment variable; in an experiment in which two treatments are administered to two large, randomly formed pools of respondents, the differences in outcome from one treatment to another still reflect both the treatment effect and the effect of respondent individuality. What these solutions *solve* is the problem of defending the claim X *causes* Y against other possible interpretations of the experiment. Random assignment of respondents to treatments, for example, does not assure equivalence of observational conditions; on the contrary, randomly formed groups of individuals must always be expected to differ at the group level to a degree determined by the size of the groups and the amount of variability from one individual to another. But random assignment of respondents to treatments, together with statistical estimation of "expected" group-to-group differences, can contribute to building a case against the argument that observed differences in outcome reflect only preexisting individual differences between the respondents given one treatment and the respondents given the other treatment.

As an example let us suppose that we have compared two teaching methods to see which is more effective. If students receiving Method A score better on a common measure of achievement than do students receiving Method B, the conclusion that Method A is better than Method B depends on our ability to answer two sorts of objections: (1) the suggestion that the groups were unequal to begin with, and (2) the suggestion that the differences between the two groups are only what one would expect as a result of average individual differences from student to student. Random assignment of students to teaching methods responds to the first of these objections, not by establishing the prior equivalence of the two groups, but by establishing that there is no good reason to believe that the group assigned to Method A started out any better than the group assigned to Method B. Statistical significance testing responds to the second objection by evaluating the observed differences against what would be expected if the objection were true—evaluating, that is, the plausibility of the idea that the observed differences in achievement could come about through random formation of groups from a common pool. When differences between treatment groups are "significant," we have not shown that the differences are free from accumulated effects of individual difference, but only that the differences are improbably large if individual differences are *all* that affect the outcomes.

Just as experimentation generally is tailored to the problem of arguing causality, the typical social scientific experiment is tailored to the problem of defending claims about causes of human response variation. This tailoring consists of the inclusion of many respondents within any observational condition, the use of random assignment of respondents to conditions, and the use of statistical procedures that evaluate apparent treatment effects against estimates of the effects of individuality. The two fundamental issues involved in defending a causal claim, the question of covariation and the question of cause, arise by virtue of what it means to say *X causes Y*, but within any substantive empirical context, these issues will take a shape determined by the characteristics of the subject matter and the state of the field.

What social scientists know about demonstrating causality has evolved in specific directions related to the special characteristics of people as objects of study.

ARGUMENTATIVE OBLIGATIONS

It is important to see that in putting forward any empirical claim a researcher takes on a certain set of obligations: first, to present a reasonable positive case in support of the claim, and second, to defend the claim against reasonable challenges.

The first set of obligations correspond roughly to what argumentation theorists label the "burden of proof." Burden of proof should be understood here as the obligation to answer such issues as might justify rejection of the claim, even in the absence of counterevidence or counterclaim. A positive case in support of a claim must give reason for believing it to be true. If the reasons given for believing a claim to be true are equally good reasons for believing a competing claim, the case cannot be said to have met its burden of proof. As a general rule, we can say that satisfaction of the burden of proof associated with a claim creates a *presumption* in favor of that claim: The claim is presumable until proven incorrect. Challenges and counterclaims take different forms depending on whether this initial burden of proof has or has not been met. When a claim is put forward without adequate grounds, it can be challenged as being no better supported than some competing claim; when a claim is given a sufficient defense, any challenge must offer positive reasons to believe that the claim is nevertheless wrong. A presumption in favor of a claim means that challenges to the claim are themselves accountable for satisfying an independent burden of proof.

The second set of obligations correspond roughly to what is often termed the "burden of rebuttal." Burden of rebuttal should be understood as involving responsiveness to counterarguments that, if true, would refute the case in support of a claim. Suppose we wish to claim, on the basis of experimental outcomes, that teaching method A is superior to teaching method B. An adequate initial defense of the claim would be a demonstration that initially indistinguishable groups of students exposed to the two methods did significantly better under Method A than under Method B. Any such claim might be challenged on the grounds that the dependent measure is not a valid indicator of achievement; to stick, such a challenge must give its own account of what is measured by the dependent measure and its own explanation of why that measure should vary with teaching method if not because Method A is superior. Unless no one really cares about the comparison between Method A and Method B, such a challenge demands a response of some sort: an effort to resolve the newly opened question of which of two accounts of the data is correct.

The distinction between these two sets of obligations—the burden of proof and the burden of rebuttal—is not sharp, and in many cases it will be impossible to say that a particular step in an argument belongs to one rather than the other. The validity of the experimenter's operationalizations of X and Y are always in principle open to challenge, but whether one needs an explicit argument for the validity of any operationalization depends on whether this is likely to be doubted in the actual concrete empirical context. The necessity for explicit defense of an operationalization declines with the transparency of its connection with the concept (its "face validity"), at least insofar as the acceptability of the causal claim is concerned. But although it is unlikely that we will be able to construct cross-situational inventories of issues constituting the researcher's burden of proof and burden of rebuttal, the distinction between the two sets of obligations is nevertheless useful, for it points to the difference between arguments that *must* be answered to establish the plausibility of a claim, and arguments that *may* have to be answered to refute counterclaims.

Notice that the burden of proof functions as a loose standard of sufficiency: a tacit understanding within a field as to what must be shown before a claim is to be taken seriously. The burden of rebuttal, on the other hand, serves as a kind of "repair mechanism" for empirical argumentation. Every empirical argument will be incomplete in an epistemological sense, and the burden of rebuttal provides for filling in of additional support at just those points in the argument that open opportunities for criticism and refutation.

Now, one important thing to notice is that a scientist's burden of proof and burden of rebuttal are limited. As Kauffeld (1989, p. 377) has pointed out, the burden of proof in any argumentative context extends only to such issues as are "worthy of consideration": "An objection may fail to be worthy of consideration, if it cannot be substantiated, if it raises a theoretical possibility which is contrary to fact, if it is entirely at odds with commonsense, and so on." There are certain sorts of objections that can be raised against any social scientific claim, but it is not necessarily the scientist's burden to respond to them. It is always possible to assert that the experimenter lied about what was observed, to insist that a sample (though randomly selected) was nonrepresentative, to doubt whether the statistics were correctly computed, and so on. But such challenges are not normally taken very seriously unless backed by some evidence. The burden of proof and the burden of rebuttal extend only to arguments that represent serious reasons to doubt the truth of a claim, and they are specifiable only against a set of presumptions, including not only substantive beliefs about the phenomena but also practical presumptions about the nature of scientific discourse and the obligations of its participants.

But to say that a scientist's burdens are limited is not to say that they are fixed or that they can be given a complete prior specification. The burden of proof involved in making a particular kind of claim depends on the state of the science, and it changes as the science progresses in its understanding of the subject matter or its understanding of the act of observation. Forms of argument considered compelling at one point in the development of a field may be shown, in subsequent analysis, to have characteristic weaknesses. For example, experiments comparing treatments with untreated controls had to be shown to be vulnerable to respondent expectancy effects, and single-blind experiments using placebos for control group respondents had to be shown to be vulnerable to experimenter expectancy effects (Orne, 1969; Rosenthal, 1969, 1976). Likewise, issues once considered controversial may be resolved "for all practical purposes," even though they represent "in principle" grounds for skepticism about any claim. For example, no contemporary social scientist wastes time challenging (or defending) the "representativeness" of samples selected at random from the population of interest, even though, in principle, a random sample can be very deviant from population characteristics, and in early applications random samples were considered unreliable (see, e.g., Porter, 1986, especially Chapter 8, or Stigler, 1986, especially Chapter 5). The development of both double-blind procedures and survey sampling methods represent alterations in the burden of proof associated with certain kinds of social scientific claims. Burden of proof evolves as scientists discover new ways that their reasoning can go wrong and as they find general practical solutions to problems previously noted.

This book is an effort to redefine the burden of proof involved in making causal claims about messages. The general approach will be to analyze the standard defense of such claims and to propose a class of challenges that the standard defense cannot meet. The sort of challenge we will be concerned with can be raised in a particularized form against a large number of the claims about message effects appearing in the experimental communication research literature, and also against a large number of the claims about message effects appearing in communication-related literatures in social psychology, advertising, and other fields concerned with social influence. The sort of problem we will be treating will be illustrated for one typical communication experiment. But it is very important to know at the outset that such particularized challenges do not represent unusual or idiosyncratic features of individual studies, but very common and general weaknesses in an approach to the design of message research. In Chapter 2, I will develop a general analysis of the standard experimental designs used in research on message effects and will show how problems follow from the very structure of the experiments.

A Case Study

The study to be analyzed (from Hosman, 1987) was concerned with the interpersonal consequences of different strategies for responding to self-disclosures. The main claim was that the acceptability of various forms of reciprocation varies according to the intimacy level of the initial disclosure: Following low-intimacy disclosures, the most acceptable responses match both topic and intimacy level, but following high-intimacy disclosures, the most acceptable responses match the topic but not the intimacy level.

These are causal claims. The effect of interest might be described generally as "judgments of message appropriateness or acceptability." The causal variables are represented as message features (or as features of the message–context relationship). Intimacy matching and topic matching are proposed causes of variations in message acceptability. This influence is asserted to be moderated by a third causal variable, a context variable that determines the kind of influence intimacy matching and topic matching will have in differing circumstances. The context variable is itself a message feature: the intimacy level of the message to which the judged message responds.

The basic experimental procedure involved presentation of two-turn dialogues to respondents, who were asked to rate the second speaker along a number of evaluative dimensions. Each dialogue consisted of an initial self-disclosure by Speaker A (varied as to its intimacy level) and a reciprocal self-disclosure by Speaker B (varied on both dimensions of matching, that is, on whether or not it matched the topic of the initial disclosure and on whether or not it matched the intimacy level of the initial disclosure). Thus the experiment involved manipulations of three variables: (1) the intimacy level of the initial self-disclosure (low versus high), manipulated through variations in the content of the first turn; (2) reciprocations of the topic (match versus mismatch between topics of the two speeches), manipulated

through variations in the content of the second turn; and (3) reciprocations of intimacy level (match versus mismatch between the intimacy levels of the two speeches), manipulated through variations
of the content of the second turn and through pairing with alternative
first turns. The various combinations of experimental conditions were
created through pairings of the two possible initiations with each of
the four possible response messages, as shown in Table 1.1.

Notice that each of the four response messages is paired with
each of the two initiations. Since the two initiation messages differ
in intimacy level, a message that matches the intimacy level of one
initiation must be a mismatch for the other initiation. On the other
hand, each response message appears either as a topic match or as a
topic mismatch, regardless of initiation, the responses having been
designed to be "on" or "off" topic for both initiations.

Ratings of Speaker B in each of the eight conditions are intended
to index the success of the various ways of responding to self-disclosure.
And the results show that these ratings varied convincingly from
dialogue to dialogue. But the claims made on the basis of the study
are nonetheless very poorly supported. Let's see why.

The main claim, that the acceptability of each of the several ways
of responding depends on the intimacy level of an initiation, breaks
down into two subclaims, the first being that low-intimacy disclosures
call for responses matched on both topic and intimacy level, and the
second being that high-intimacy disclosures call for responses matched
on topic but *not* on intimacy level. For the main claim and for each

TABLE 1.1. Experimental Conditions as Combinations of an Initial Disclosure and a
Response Disclosure

Intimacy of initiation	Intimacy of response	Topic	
		Match	Mismatch
Low	Match	Initiation 1 Response 1	Initiation 1 Response 2
	Mismatch	Initiation 1 Response 3	Initiation 1 Response 4
High	Match	Initiation 2 Response 3	Initiation 2 Response 4
	Mismatch	Initiation 2 Response 1	Initiation 2 Response 2

of the two subclaims, the analytic question we must pose is whether we can take the data presented in the report as grounds for believing the claims to be true. The subclaims are easier to analyze, so we will begin with them, then return to the main claim.

Consider the first subclaim, that following low-intimacy disclosures, the most acceptable of the four response types is the one involving matching on both intimacy level and topic. To support this claim, it is necessary to establish that responses of one particular type are better than responses of other types following initiations of a certain type. The experiment uses a single concrete narrative to represent each type of disclosure, and this is the source of a very serious weakness in its case. The data do in fact show that following the low-intimacy initiation, the available responses are ordered from best to worst as follows: the response matching both topic and intimacy level, the response matching on intimacy level but mismatching on topic, the response matching on topic but mismatching on intimacy level, and the response mismatching on both topic and intimacy level. But the question is, can we account for this ordering without invoking concepts like topic and intimacy matching?

If the differences in acceptability among the response messages are to be interpreted as evidence of the effects of topic and intimacy matching, then the individual messages used to represent each type should have no important differences, one from another, other than differences in intimacy level and topicality. This can be directly assessed through examination of the content of the response messages. The low-intimacy initiation was a brief narrative about meeting a science fiction writer in a bar, and the four response messages were, respectively, a brief narrative about meeting and conversing with a stranger in an airport, a brief narrative about the lifestyle associated with working at a "night spot," a brief narrative about being "hustled" (successfully) by women in bars, and a brief confession about involvement in drug trafficking.

We can insert this content into our abstract representation of the design, selecting only those cells relevant to the first of the causal claims; this is shown in Table 1.2.

Here is the analytic question: *To establish the superiority of responses matched on both aspects of reciprocation following low-intimacy disclosures, is it sufficient to show that one of the four concrete response narratives is better than the others following this particular initiation?* No: One quite good rival hypothesis is that the four responses vary intrinsically in what they say about the character of the speaker. Each of these responses

TABLE 1.2. Experimental Dialogues Involving the Low-Intimacy Initiation

Intimacy of initiation	Intimacy of response	Topic	
		Match	Mismatch
Low	Match	Sci-fi writer Stranger in airport	Sci-fi writer Nightspot lifestyle
Low	Mismatch	Sci-fi writer Being hustled by women	Sci-fi writer Smuggling drugs

has rich content information about the life of the speaker; they appear in full in the original report and in very brief summary here. Response 1, for example, portrays the speaker as both well traveled and friendly, while Response 4 suggests that the speaker is an habitual criminal. Surely it is no surprise that Response 1 is considered vastly more acceptable than Response 4—after all, independent of topic, being friendly would seem better than being criminal, and surely the unacceptability of confiding one's criminal conduct has more to do with the evaluation of the conduct than with evaluation of the act of confiding.

The rival hypothesis is that ratings of acceptability for the four response messages do not depend on the intimacy and topic matching features, but on a different feature, one that might be described as "social acceptability of the behavior disclosed." Such a variable is conceptually quite independent of intimacy level: A very intimate disclosure may be either positive or negative in what it reveals about the discloser, and the same is true for nonintimate disclosures. To pose a serious challenge to the causal claim offered by the experimenter, a competing hypothesis of this kind must give a plausible account of the data. In this case, the competing hypothesis has great plausibility, since the best-liked response was the story of talking with a stranger in an airport and the least-liked response was the confession of drug smuggling.

Table 1.3 summarizes a comparison between the original interpretation of the results and the interpretation suggested by the rival hypothesis. The four response messages are arranged from most to least acceptable with acceptability measured in terms of respondents' ratings. The original descriptions of the disclosures (in terms of topic and intimacy matching) appear in one column, and the rival description (in terms of social acceptability of the behavior disclosed) in another column. Both descriptions are problematic, but both can be bolstered through such things as independent coding of the messages for level

TABLE 1.3. Two Alternative Accounts of the Data Offered as Support for Claims about Responses to Low-Intimacy Initiations

Response narrative	Intimacy/Topic	Character information
Stranger in airport	Match/Match	Positive
Night-spot lifestyle	Match/Mismatch	Neutral to negative
Being hustled by women	Mismatch/Match	Negative
Smuggling drugs	Mismatch/Mismatch	Negative

of intimacy, topical similarity, and general positivity. Shortly, we will consider the bearing of the study's manipulation check data on the plausibility of the rival description.

Notice that both descriptions may be correct, and, in fact, both appear to be reasonable classifications of the narratives. The important question to consider is which description gives a more plausible account of the ordering of narratives from most to least acceptable? The point is that if the narratives do in fact differ in intrinsic acceptability—by virtue of what they reveal about the speaker—it is not reasonable to claim that their differences in rated acceptability depend on matching of the features of the preceding turn.

Now, we could run through the same sort of examination for the second subclaim, that high-intimacy disclosures call for responses matched on topic but not on intimacy. The high-intimacy initiation was a brief narrative about a sexual encounter in a bar, and the four response narratives, though the same as before, appeared in different cells when paired with the high-intimacy initiation, as shown in Table 1.4.

The results seemed to show that different message types were preferred following high-intimacy initiations than following low intimacy initiations. Whereas for the first analysis the best response was the one matching on both intimacy level and topic, for the second

TABLE 1.4. Experimental Dialogues Involving the High-Intimacy Initiation

Intimacy of initiation	Intimacy of response	Topic	
		Match	Mismatch
High	Match	Sexual adventure Being hustled by women	Sexual adventure Smuggling drugs
High	Mismatch	Sexual adventure Stranger in airport	Sexual adventure Night spot lifestyle

analysis the best response was the one matching on topic, but not on intimacy level. However, again we must examine the evidence more closely. As can be seen from Table 1.5, the response judged best was the same in both cases, specifically, the narrative about chatting with a stranger in an airport. Table 1.5 repeats the comparison between the original and the rival descriptions of the disclosures, to allow further comparison of the hypothesis that ratings of acceptability depend on matching and the hypothesis that ratings of acceptability depend on information about the speaker's character.

The weakness in the evidence for the claims about matching is highlighted by the presence of a very strong rival explanation of the results. But should elimination of this rival claim be considered part of the burden of proof involved in making any claim about why responses to disclosures vary in acceptability? The answer is yes and no. The burden of proof obviously cannot include elimination of all individual rival hypotheses, but it can include an obligation to show that the responses do not differ intrinsically in acceptability. One way of establishing this would be to obtain ratings of the acceptability of the various response measures, independently of any initiation message, and to show that "out of context" the four response messages are judged equally acceptable. Such ratings were in fact obtained (as part of a manipulation check), but unfortunately they established not the equality of the four responses, but their inequality. The report contains evidence that the four response narratives do differ intrinsically in acceptability: Removed from context, so that there is no information at all on either dimension of matching, the messages differed significantly in their acceptability. The story about chatting with a stranger in an airport was perceived as significantly more acceptable than any of the other three (these three failing to differ significantly among themselves). These data give exceptionally strong support to the rival description of the narratives in terms of intrinsic acceptability of the information conveyed.

TABLE 1.5. Two Alternative Accounts of the Data Offered as Support for Claims about Responses to High-Intimacy Initiations

Response narrative	Intimacy/Topic	Character information
Stranger in airport	Mismatch/Match	Positive
Being hustled by women	Match/Match	Negative
Smuggling drugs	Match/Mismatch	Negative
Night-spot lifestyle	Mismatch/Mismatch	Neutral to negative

Approaching the study's claims argumentatively, it is clear that there is a substantial weakness in the case. Specifically, the variations in ratings of the four responses can be very plausibly interpreted as reflecting nothing more than the intrinsic differences in acceptability of the acts disclosed. Let us review the evidence for the rival hypothesis. The results of the manipulation check suggest that quite independently of interactional context, Response 1 reflects best on the speaker, with Responses 2, 3, and 4 indiscriminately worse. Following the low-intimacy initiation, Response 1 was judged significantly more acceptable than the other three, though Response 4 was also differentiated as being significantly worse than Responses 2 and 3. Following the high-intimacy initiation, Response 1 was again judged significantly more acceptable than the other three, with Responses 2, 3, and 4 judged negatively and without significant differentiation. To assert, as the author does, that high-intimacy disclosures call for topical continuations but not reciprocation of intimacy, while low-intimacy disclosures call for topical continuations and reciprocation of intimacy is quite un-justified, for the data present a solid case that the four responses examined as representatives of each class are in fact intrinsically different in attractiveness, regardless of the characteristics of the prior remark and, indeed, regardless of whether there is any prior remark at all. The data confirm a perfectly ordinary expectation that an admission of having chatted with a stranger is considerably less discrediting than an admission of having engaged in any sort of illegal or morally questionable behavior. The relevant data are arrayed in Table 1.6. The acceptability of each response message relative to the others, controlling context, can be read down the columns; the acceptability of a response across contexts, which can be read along rows of the table, is not directly relevant to the two subclaims considered so far.

What about the more general claim that the acceptability of a response type depends on the characteristics of the initiating turn? Even if we cannot substantiate any claim about the specific type of response called for by any given type of initiation, perhaps we can at least establish that self-disclosures differing in intimacy level have *some* sort of effect on the acceptability of responses. From Table 1.6, it can be seen that the acceptability of some of the response messages was indeed influenced by the initiation messages. For example, both the narrative about chatting with a stranger in an airport and the narrative about drug dealing were rated more positively when paired with the high-intimacy initiation than when paired with the low-intimacy initiation, while the narrative about tending bar was rated more positively when paired with the low-intimacy initiation than

TABLE 1.6. Acceptability of Responses across Contexts

Response message	No context[a]	Initiation 1[b]	Initiation 2[b]
Stranger in airport	46.3	.700	1.221
Night-spot lifestyle	34.5	.252	−.602
Being hustled by women	34.8	−.151	−.159
Smuggling drugs	32.6	−.854	−.309

[a] Means derived from the manipulation check, computed over summed ratings on eight social attractiveness items.
[b] Social attractiveness factor score computed as a weighted composite of eight items.

with the high-intimacy initiation. That is, while the two specific subclaims are essentially unsupported, it is clear that the acceptability of a response is somehow dependent on the discourse context. But it should be clear by now that any attempt to account for these differences in generic terms—any claim, that is, about the effects of the *intimacy level* of the initiation on any or all of the responses—will be vulnerable to the same sort of critique that we have leveled against the subclaims: Specifically, we might note that the two initiations differ in content dimensions other than intimacy, in the same way that the response messages differ in content dimensions other than matching.

Recall that the low-intimacy initiation involved a story about meeting a science fiction writer in a bar, while the high-intimacy initiation involved a story about a sexual encounter with a strange woman in a bar. Is intimacy level the only message feature that differentiates these two messages? No. Among other differences between the two disclosures, three strike me as particularly likely to have an effect on the interpretation and evaluation of any subsequent message: general interest value, general clarity of point, and general information about speaker's character. For example, a relatively uninteresting response message following a very interesting narrative may look poorer by comparison than the same message following a less interesting narrative. So although it is possible to say that the acceptability of some responses depends on the conversational context, it is not possible to say what feature(s) of the conversational context are the source of this dependency.

Not much can be salvaged of the study's claim: only the relatively vacuous point that the acceptability of a conversational turn *may* depend on some feature of what has preceded it. Once we try to specify *what* features of the turn or its context are important in determining the acceptability of a response, we find the structure of the experiment inadequate to the defense of any one hypothesis against an array of other equally good hypotheses. For both the initiation messages and the response messages, the experiment *confounds* the message features of interest (intimacy level, intimacy matching, topic matching) with a large number of uncontrolled and unconsidered content differences among the disclosures used to represent each type.

The closing paragraphs of the report make reference to the possibility of some sort of confounding of message content with "topic reciprocity." That variations in message content are confounded, not only with the topic reciprocity dimension, but also with the intimacy reciprocity dimension, is a fact. The implications to be drawn from this fact depend upon whether the content variations can account for the differences in ratings of the dialogues. It seems clear that they can. To build a strong case for the original claims, it would be necessary to show that the differences in ratings of dialogues are *not* attributable to these uncontrolled content variations.

The claims offered as conclusions from this study carry with them a readily identifiable burden of proof. The experiment and its outcomes fail to meet this burden of proof. The claims themselves may be true or false, but to evaluate them will require a different sort of study. Specifically, the claim could be bolstered through confirmation of the patterns observed with different message content, and especially with message content in which "general" acceptability is equated. Strategies for repairing designs of this type are discussed fully in Chapters 3 and 4.

The Source of the Problem

Is it possible to say where the study went wrong? In the particular experiment we have been discussing, all of the problems arise from a common source, namely the use of a single concrete narrative to represent each disclosure type. The individual narratives vary in too many ways other than intimacy level and topicality to permit any categorical interpretation of the differences in their rated acceptability. Like many other experiments in communication, this study errs in not giving any serious consideration to how individual messages stand in relation to message classes, a central issue addressed throughout this book. Paradoxically, it is inadequate attention to the special problems posed by messages as objects of study that is the source of the major methodological problems of message effects research.

Most of the time in experimental communication research, messages have been treated, improperly, as operationalizations of message variables. An operationalization of any variable should be a procedure for embodying a concept, interchangeable with any other defensible procedure for embodying the same concept. Treatments applied to messages may properly be seen as operationalizations of message variables if "treatment" is understood rather abstractly as a procedure for generating the messages or for altering certain of their features. But messages themselves as concrete texts should not be understood as operationalizations. Instead, they should ordinarily be understood as *representatives* of message types. They are *sample instantiations* of a treatment or sample instantiations of a category. This is an extremely important point. It suggests that the role of an individual message within an experiment is more like the role of an individual respondent than it is like the role of a measuring instrument.

Like human respondents, messages present certain kinds of methodological difficulties for experimentation, but the difficulties messages present have not been systematically analyzed. When individual messages are treated as direct operationalizations of message variables rather than as samples from message classes or sample instantiations of a contrast, the resulting experiments will not usually support any nonvacuous claim about message effects. Unless we are willing to give up the effort to discover things about messages as classes, we are going to have to develop some new ways of thinking about messages and some new ways of researching them. Systematic attention to messages as objects of study must lead to a redefinition of the burden of proof attached to claims about message effects.

SOME GENERAL PRESUPPOSITIONS ABOUT MESSAGES

What can we say about messages and message classes that might affect the way we go about the study of messages? As a starting point for discussion of design and analysis issues, let us consider two fundamental premises that seem to follow from contemporary theories of language and communication.

Premise 1: Every message is unique and every message description is incomplete.

When we take an interest in any message class, we assume that all objects that may be seen as members of that class share in common the feature or features that define the class. But the members of the class are in other ways very diverse, and each one has some uniqueness about it. Another way of putting this is to say that messages cannot be "decomposed" into a list of values on some "master list" of message variables (Ellis, 1982). In principle, the ways in which we might choose to describe or classify any message are inexhaustible (D. O'Keefe, 1990), and any description or classification of a message variable will be only a *partial* description relative to some current interest. This innocuous premise has some extremely important consequences for message-centered research methods.

Consider the class of "negative political ads." The members of the class must all be advertisements, aimed at generating votes for a specific political candidate, and exhibiting at least one negative statement about the candidate's opponent. However, in other respects the members of the class are likely to be quite diverse. They will vary in all sorts of ways: in whether or not the favored candidate is mentioned, in whether the negative information is implicit or explicit, in accuracy of the negative information, in familiarity and importance of the issue addressed, in campaign context, in timeliness, in quality of production, in length, in language intensity, in argumentative structure, in use of caricature, in use of slogans, and so on.

Or consider a class of messages central to the case study considered earlier in this chapter: self-disclosures. The members of this class must reveal "privileged" information about the speaker, and presumably, the revelation of this information must be the point of the utterance. We can define certain dimensions along which members of the class differ, such as intimacy level and topic, but even if these dimensions exhaust our theoretical interests in self-disclosures, they do not exhaust the communicatively important differences between one self-disclosure and another. We saw this concretely in the case study. Other dimensions of difference among self-disclosures might include the favorability of the information disclosed, the interest value of the disclosure as a narrative, the clarity of the point being made in the disclosure, interactional purpose, narrative structure, point of view, evaluativeness, self-consciousness, syntactic complexity, lexical diversity, language intensity, length, imagery, humor, fit with ongoing interactional episode, relevance to the speaker's relationship to the addressee, and so on. Even these do not exhaust the differences between one disclosure and another that might make a difference to some dimension of response: Disclosures differ along an indefinitely large number of dimensions, only some of which are available to us within the current state of our theorizing about language and communication.

The judgment that any particular object does or does not belong to the class obviously does not exhaust the things that might be said about the object. In fact, each message, message element, or exchange of messages within a class must have some features that distinguish it from all other members of the class, whether these be text features, performance features, contextual features, or whatever. Messages treated as members of a class are like people treated as members of a class: To say that any given message is a negative ad or that any given message is a high-intimacy self-disclosure is to give only a partial description based on our current interests, just as to say that a person is female or cognitively complex or the second of four children is to give only a partial description based on our current interests.

Basic textbooks in communication theory often stress that messages are unique and individual. This is not to say that messages cannot be systematically described or classified, but only that descriptions and classifications of messages with respect to any finite set of dimensions will be *incomplete* in principle.

One way to understand this point is by way of an analogy with our descriptions and classifications of people. We do not assume that even a very complex description of a person or a very fine classification of a set of people exhausts all of what might be said about the person or what might be done to differentiate one person from another. If we describe a person in terms of a great many attributes (say gender, height, weight, race, national origin, religious background and preference, marital status and history, educational level, income, occupational status, political affiliation and preference, intelligence, extroversion, dogmatism, egocentrism, altruism, tendency to self-monitor, and cognitive complexity), we have still given only a very partial description of the person. And we presume that that will be true even if we include an evaluation of the person against *every* dimension that is currently considered relevant to social research in any of its various fields and subfields.

Classifications of messages, even very fine classifications, are incomplete descriptions in the same sense. Suppose we classify self-disclosures not only as to whether they are high or low in intimacy and on or off topic, but also as to whether they are short or long, syntactically simple or complex, selfconscious or unselfconscious, evaluative or nonevaluative, humorous or pathetic, relevant or irrelevant to the speaker–addressee relationship, and so on. Such a classification remains incomplete in the sense that messages sharing a common classification on all currently included dimensions will still be recognizably different from one another—and therefore incompletely described by the current classification.

The methodological implication to be drawn from this assumption can only be previewed at this point, but will be fully developed by the end of the book. Messages used in experiments should usually be treated as respondents are treated: not as embodiments of the values of a variable, but as representatives of a class or as instantiations of a contrast. The uniqueness of the individual message means that any one message treated as a representative of a type differs from other possible representatives of the type. A single concrete message is best considered a sample of one from a class of other messages sharing the features that define the class, but otherwise differing in any number of ways. As with human respondents, we will not normally be able to draw conclusions about the characteristics of a class based on observation of single cases.

Our methodology for dealing with messages as objects of study will have to incorporate some effort to come to terms with uniqueness and within-class variability. Two obvious possibilities suggest themselves. One is to try to isolate the message variables of interest to us from all other differences, by "controlling" or "holding constant" all features of individual messages other than the feature whose effects we want to measure. Trying to avoid extraneous variations between or among experimental conditions is always desirable, but a solution of this form is not well tailored to the fundamental problems of a methodology for message effects research. This sort of strategy presumes an ability to identify and control all of the message features that make a difference or might make a difference to our dependent variable, and we neither have this ability now nor have we any realistic chance of gaining this ability in the foreseeable future. The other possibility is to seek the differences between message classes or the effects of message variables at an aggregate level, as averages across large samples of messages of the types defined by the research problem. This strategy involves no repudiation of experimental control, but only a recognition of its limits. With messages, as with people, experimental control must be supplemented by a strategy of "replication," that is, a strategy of multiple representation within any observational condition. The first of these contrasted strategies is the practical consequence of treating messages as operationalizations of message variables, while the second follows from the shift to a view of messages as sample instantiations of a class or type. In subsequent chapters, I will try to show the profound inadequacies of any solution based on a view of messages as operationalizations, and to outline how and why a solution based on a view of messages as samples is better.

Premise 2: Message classes are abstract types rather than concrete collections of things.

Treating messages as sample instantiations of a type draws attention to issues of representation and representativeness. Extending the general idea that methods must be tailored to the properties of the object of study, it will be necessary to come to terms with the ways in which messages may be taken as representative of message classes.

Message classes are not large sets of cases, but abstract categories whose members are recognizable once produced, but whose total membership is neither enumerable in practice nor exhaustible in principle. A message class will have, except in certain special cases, an infinite number of members.

Consider the class of negative political ads. This class is a subclass of all political ads, and some number of its members can be found in archival records of past political campaigns. The University of Oklahoma's Political Commercial Archive, a very comprehensive collection of televised political advertisements, contains many examples of negative political advertising. But these examples do not define the class of negative political ads. The class includes not only all those commercials we can recover, but also all of those previously broadcast and lost, all of those that *will* be broadcast, and all of those that *could* be produced and broadcast. In making a claim about the effect of negative political advertising, we are not merely summarizing response to some finite collection of ads but predicting consequences of the use of this strategy.

Notice that conventional wisdom pertaining to representativeness cannot be extended to messages as objects of study: As a practical fact, we cannot apply random sampling procedures to message classes, as we can to human populations with specifiable membership. Virtually all samples from message classes will look like convenience samples, selected arbitrarily or haphazardly. We know a good deal about how to justify generalizations from samples drawn in certain ways from populations that amount to concrete collections of objects. But we know less, at least at a reflective level, about how to justify generalizations from samples drawn in arbitrary or haphazard ways (even though this is by far the more common route to generalization in social science experimentation). An articulated position on generalization, one detached from random sampling methods, is central to any specialized communication research methodology, and perhaps to all of the experimental social sciences.

Another consequence of this fact (that message classes are abstract types rather than concrete collections) is that message classes can be defined and redefined as we progress in our study of a problem. Our conceptualization of any message class is our own creation, subject to change as we go along. This means that the relationship between a message class and a message sample may or may not be best understood as a set/subset relationship. The class may be considered instead to be implicit in the cases taken to exemplify it. This shift of viewpoint might be partially accomplished by speaking of messages not as *samples from a class* but as *exemplars of a class*. When we speak of research on message effects, the message class to which the claim refers is not always knowable in advance, but sometimes emergent from the very effort of representation. I am suggesting that the class of interest must sometimes, perhaps always, be reconstructed (at a reflective level) from the nature of the messages used to represent it. For example, if we are interested in whether one-sided or two-sided argumentation is more effective, presumably we want to know which of the two strategies to prefer in precisely those cases in which it is possible to use either one. Messages taken as good exemplars of such a situation do not *select* from a class of interest, but serve to *define* the class of interest. This is an unusual way of thinking about samples, but one that is coherent and useful within a general view of research as argumentative. We will see later how this way of thinking can introduce important subordinate steps in arguments for generality of an effect.

ORGANIZATION OF THE BOOK

The point of this book is to develop a systematic approach to experimental design involving messages or message variables. The systematic basis for its proposals is a view of research as an argumentative process in which claims are put forward and defended against actual or potential counterclaims. We will begin in Chapter 2 by considering the abstract structure of the typical empirical argument offered in support of a claim about message effects. The typical argument (like the specific case we considered earlier) contains a weakness so general and so profound as to require a redefinition of the burden of proof associated with such claims. Chapters 3 and 4 offer a basic design strategy that is responsive to this redefined burden of proof.

Chapters 5 and 6 concern the statistical analysis of designs such as those recommended in Chapters 3 and 4. The statistical analysis of an experiment will be considered argumentatively, as a way of generating responses to certain kinds of questions and challenges that might be raised against a causal claim. Within this general framework, alternative forms of analysis will be considered and compared, and certain controversial issues will be thoroughly reviewed. Chapter 7 will explore sampling and generalization, with the aim of identifying issues attached to claims of generality. Strategies for arguing generality will be discussed and some concrete sampling procedures described.

The concluding chapter will return to the point previewed in the opening pages of this chapter: the idea that a disciplined study of any subject matter should develop specialized methodology built on carefully examined assumptions about the requirements of empirical demonstration and the objects of study themselves. In that context, I will offer an analysis of the structure of empirical arguments about message effects, and outline a position on the burden of proof that such arguments must shoulder. Within this context, it will be seen that the specifics of the proposals offered in Chapters 2–7 are contingent, not necessary. Although they offer solutions to some of the argumentative problems we face, they are not always complete solutions, and they are never the only possible solutions.

TWO

Threats to Validity in Standard Experimental Designs

The characteristic problem of research on message effects is to establish relationships between message features and process or outcome variables. Let us begin by surveying briefly the sorts of research questions with which we will be concerned. Typical problems include such questions as the following:

1. *Questions about the relative effectiveness of alternative persuasive strategies.* Do appeals based on threat or fear arousal increase in persuasiveness as a function of increases in the magnitude of the threat? What effect does intense language have on message effectiveness? Is two-sided argumentation more persuasive than one-sided argumentation, and, if so, are there limiting conditions on the applicability of the strategy?

2. *Questions about mass media processes and effects.* Is newsworthiness a function of deviance from the expected? Does pornography cause violence against women? Do negative political ads help or hurt a candidate's campaign?

3. *Questions about the relative effectiveness of interpersonal communication strategies.* What is the most effective way to respond to a complaint? In offering comfort to someone in distress, is it more effective to focus on the feelings of distress or to try to distract the distressed

person from preoccupation with the feelings? What is the most effective type of "account," when a person has been charged with any sort of inappropriate conduct?

4. *Questions about the personal and social consequences of communicative behaviors not considered strategic.* How do perceptions of a speaker's attractiveness and competence vary with expression of emotion? Does self-disclosure promote perceptions of closeness? Do awkward silences in conversation affect observers' perceptions of the conversationalists' competence?

5. *Questions about discourse structure and discourse processing.* What text features contribute to comprehension and recall of a message? How does thematization in discourse contribute to interpretation? What kinds of utterance-to-utterance linkages affect the overall coherence of discourse? How does "literal meaning" enter into the interpretation of "indirect speech acts"?

The first three groups of questions, those concerned with the relationship between communicative choices and communicative outcomes, will be of particular concern to us in the development of a specialized methodology, for they call attention to just what is at stake in research on message variables. Research prompted by these questions aims for establishment of general principles of the form "Strategy A is more effective than Strategy B in pursuing outcome O." Such principles have obvious practical consequences; they amount to recommendations. We can always gain useful perspective when evaluating research on such questions by asking ourselves whether a communicator would or would not be well-advised to *act* on the proposed principle. A communicator would be well-advised to act on such a principle only if there were good reason to believe that it is true.

A proposition like "Strategy A is more effective than Strategy B" appearing in the research literature is an empirical claim in need of evidence. Experimental findings should be considered as evidence and evaluated accordingly.

Notice that within each of the classes of research problems mentioned above, message features are considered as possible sources of influence and audience responses to messages are considered as effects or registers of effects. The interest behind the question may be very concrete and practical, aimed for example at giving advice to persuaders or at helping people to develop better interpersonal communication skills. Or the interest may be theoretical, aimed at testing a hypothetical model of comprehension or a hypothesis about discourse structure. The common element in the research problems addressed by this book is the emphasis on message features as influences on processes or outcomes.

The purpose of this chapter is to examine the "standard" experimental designs used to answer questions of these types, the designs that have typically been used and that are generally accepted within the research community as strategies for generating answers to these types of questions. The vast majority of experiments on message variables use one of two basic designs. I will describe these two basic designs and discuss their structural weaknesses.

The discussion to follow is straightforwardly critical. The communication research literature contains a great number of claims about message effects, the vast majority of which are supported by evidence generated within one of the two standard designs. But these designs do not allow for strong arguments. Most of the time, the causal claims put forward as interpretations of the experiment's outcomes are not in fact justified in any reasonable sense by the data. While it is the interpretation of the experiments—that is, the claims advanced from them—that are faulty, it will shortly become clear that experiments conducted using the standard designs are generally incapable of producing a strong case in support of the claims communication researchers aim to put forward. These experiments are structurally maladapted to the research problems they are intended to address.

The two standard designs—which I will term *the unreplicated categorical comparison design* and *the unreplicated treatment comparison design*—differ primarily in the way the message variable is conceptualized and operationalized. In the first, the categorical comparison design, the objective is to compare two or more distinct categories of messages. The message variable is some distinction among messages that defines categories or types. For example, we might be interested in evaluating which is the more offensive form of humor, humor based on ethnic stereotypes or humor based on gender stereotypes. The message variable of interest might be described as "basis for humor" and its two values (for the purpose of the experiment) are "ethnic stereotype" and "gender stereotype." These values define distinct classes of messages. Or we might be interested in whether different types of self-disclosure (say, disclosures of actions vs. disclosures of feelings) have differing consequences on feelings of intimacy between speaker and hearer. Then the message variable, "self-disclosure type," would have two values, "actions" and "feelings," defining two classes of self-disclosing messages.

The second design, the treatment comparison design, has as its objective a comparison between strategic options available within a fixed context. That is, it aims to evaluate the consequences of varying particular features within a given message. This sort of variable can take the form of a "treatment" applied to an individual message to modify the message in some limited way. If we are interested in the relationship between language intensity and persuasion, we can think of language intensity as a feature that can be modified within a message whose basic argumentative structure and content remain the same. Thus, language intensity is a message variable that can be varied within a message, rather than a variable that serves to classify any given message as to its level of intensity.

The distinction between categorical comparisons and treatment comparisons is drawn for convenience in discussing different sorts of design problems arising from different sorts of research questions. The distinction boils down to whether we are interested in a message variable that suggests a classification of messages or in a message variable that suggests a choice of features to be embedded within a given message. Variables conceptualized as malleable features of a message can be applied as treatments to "controlled" message contents, while variables conceptualized in terms of message classification cannot.

Certain message variables might be conceptualized as either classifications or treatments. For example, if we wish to compare two types of persuasive strategy (say, an appeal based on altruism and an appeal based on self-interest), one might suppose that an appeal is either of one type or the other, and hence that the "strategy type" variable falls into the first class. However, it is possible to think of the appeals not as overall message strategies but as elements in a larger framework: in an extended persuasive message involving, say, an appeal plus a proposal plus a series of suggested actions. Then the appeal might be considered an element of the message, or a treatment varied within the message.

The fuzziness of the distinction between the two research situations need not alarm us, because the standard designs associated with both types of research questions share a common problem: They attempt to draw general conclusions from observation of a single message of each type required by the experiment. This is what is meant by the use of "unreplicated" in connection with each design. As can perhaps be anticipated from the critical analysis of the self-disclosure experiment in Chapter 1, this reliance on single-message instantiations of categorical contrasts or treatments opens any nonvacuous interpretation of the result to serious challenges and counterclaims. The problems with these designs are not, of course, insoluble. In Chapters 3 and 4 I will offer simple design solutions to the problems identified in this chapter. These design solutions, tailored to a burden of proof implicit in the critique of the standard designs, will be examined for their ability to generate stronger arguments in support of claims about message effects.

UNREPLICATED CATEGORICAL COMPARISONS

Experiments on message variables aimed at comparing two or more categories of messages—usually in terms of response to messages of each type—generally involve randomly formed groups of human subjects responding to a message of one category or the other. The standard design is to use one message to represent each category. This design appears in extended form, for example, in a large number of experiments on the relationship between interpersonal situation and interpersonal compliance-gaining strategy (e.g., Miller, Boster, Roloff, & Seibold, 1977; Lustig & King, 1980; McLaughlin, Cody, & Robey, 1980; a very detailed critique of these studies appears in Jackson & Backus, 1982).

The basic structure of an unreplicated categorical comparison is given in Figure 2.1. The independent variable defines two or more classes of messages. Each level of the independent variable is represented by one message. The dependent variable is some response made by human respondents. Often, these respondents will be sorted into several separate groups, one group to a message, as shown in Part A of the figure. An obvious variation on this prototype would be to present each message to each respondent (a repeated-measures version of the unreplicated categorical comparison), as shown in Part B. The important thing to notice in both versions is the one-to-one pairing of individual messages with message categories.

To concretize the discussion, let us imagine an experiment in which we want to determine which of two types of jokes is more offensive to a certain sort of audience, jokes based on ethnic stereotypes or jokes based on gender stereotypes. The message variable of interest is "basis for humor," and its values are "ethnic stereotype" and "gender stereotype." The outcome of interest is offensiveness, which we will measure by asking some number of people to report the degree to which they are offended by each joke. In an unreplicated categorical comparison, the actual design of the study would involve comparison of responses to a single ethnic-based joke and a single gender-based joke as representatives of their respective classes. A difference in response

Independent Groups Version

Category 1	Message 1	Person 1
		Person 2
		.
		.
		Person n
Category 2	Message 2	Person $n + 1$
		Person $n + 2$
		.
		.
		Person $2n$
Category 3	Message 3	Person $2n + 1$
		Person $2n + 2$
		.
		.
		Person $3n$

Repeated Measures Version

Category 1	Message 1	Person 1
		Person 2
		.
		.
		Person n
Category 2	Message 2	Person 1
		Person 2
		.
		.
		Person n
Category 3	Message 3	Person 1
		Person 2
		.
		.
		Person n

FIGURE 2.1. Unreplicated categorical comparsion designs. Note: n = the number of persons per cell; in Design type A, different people respond to each message, while in Design type B, the same people respond to all of the message.

to the two jokes would be interpreted as an effect of the basis for the joke.

For this example the problems involved in an unreplicated categorical comparison are extremely obvious. To infer that ethnic-based jokes are more or less offensive than gender-based jokes from a difference between two individual jokes is roughly comparable to inferring that women are more or less persuasive than men on the basis of a comparison between Jane and John. Just as any Jane-and-John pair will differ in many respects other than gender, any two jokes will differ in many respects other than the basis for the humor, and this makes any categorical inference from the comparison quite shaky. No one would actually undertake a comparison between the two types of jokes in so obviously inadequate a manner. Yet the very same design is often applied to comparisons among message types, and although the weaknesses of the comparison are usually more subtle than in our example, they are nevertheless very serious. The experiment considered as a case study in Chapter 1 is a complex variation on the unreplicated categorical comparison, and the problems that arise in efforts to interpret its results are entirely typical within the communication research literature.

We can identify two sorts of threats to validity that plague unreplicated categorical comparisons: *case–category confounding* and *concealed insufficiency of data.* We will explore each of these in detail.

Case-Category Confounding

A conclusion is threatened by case–category confounding when the evidence on which it rests allows no analytic separation between the properties of a category of objects and the individual properties of the cases belonging to the category (Kay & Richter, 1977). In research on message effects, case–category confounding occurs when conclusions about categorical differences are drawn from comparisons among individual members of the contrasted categories—designs in which a single example represents each category of interest.

Case–category confounding is the fundamental problem with our hypothetical study on the two types of offensive jokes. This problem affects any conclusion about classes based on comparisons among single representatives of each class. In such a design, the characteristics of the class and the characteristics of the case chosen to represent the class are said to be *confounded* in this sense: There is no way to untangle the effects of the class from the effects that are peculiar to cases within the class.

Let's consider another example. Suppose we wish to determine which of several persuasive strategy types is most effective in getting people to contribute money to charity. The standard design for investigating this would be to construct an example of each strategy type in the form of a concrete persuasive appeal, to present each persuasive appeal to a certain number of possible donors, and to compare the amounts of money received in response to each appeal. For example, if the intended comparison is between appeals based on altruism and appeals based on self-interest, the exemplifications might look like this:

Altruistic: "Charitable giving is the one means by which each of us can work directly to ease human misery and despair. Think about those who so desperately need your help. Your gifts can help to feed the hungry, house the homeless, and heal the sick. Much suffering can be relieved or eliminated through simple acts of human kindness and sharing. Please give what you can from what you have."

Self-interested: "Charitable giving is an act that has benefits for the giver as well as for the recipient. Money you give to charity goes directly to solving problems you consider important, whether those be environmental protection, animal rights, or the search for a cure for cancer. In giving to charitable causes, you take direct action to improve the quality of life for yourself and your community."

Now, one can envision circumstances in which it will be important to make a choice, not between two *strategies*, but between two actual, concrete messages. Perhaps we must decide how to spend a fixed advertising budget on either one or the other of these two brief messages. An experimental comparison between the two actual messages is a perfectly reasonable basis for choice. But that is not the usual purpose of experimentation using message materials. The *usual* purpose is to find out about the relative effectiveness of two or more strategies, considered abstractly, with no single application in mind. If the purpose behind the comparison between the two messages above is to try to find out which is more effective, altruism or self-interest, then the two messages are not at all reasonable as a basis for decision making.

Let's suppose that these two brief messages result in very different levels of giving when presented to two apparently equivalent audiences. We can certainly draw reasonable conclusions about which of the two messages is the more effective, but we cannot draw any reasonable conclusions about which of the two abstract strategies is the more effective. The two messages differ not only in whether they use altruism or self-interest as the underlying motivation, but also in many other obvious and non-obvious ways. No conclusion drawn at the level of abstract categorical differences can be said to be supported by the outcomes, because there are an indefinitely large number of categorical differences between the two messages, and every one of these explains the data as well as any other. Notice that among other things, the two messages differ in the *form* of the closing appeal: The first makes a direct request in imperative form, while the second makes an indirect request cast in the form of a statement about the consequences of the requested action. Or alternatively, notice the differences in content: Different charities are suggested by the two messages. So, if we assert that it is appeal type (altruism vs. self-interest) that accounts for differences in giving, it can be countered that it is not appeal type, but appeal form or appeal content that results in more giving for one message than for the other.

Perhaps it will occur to you that some of these rival hypotheses could be eliminated through some "control" of message features other than those we wish to compare. We have, in fact, controlled one aspect of the message, namely, its basic persuasive purpose. But this control has limits because of the very nature of the variable. You can evaluate these limits for yourself by trying to write two persuasive messages to represent the contrast between altruism and self-interest, or by trying to write two jokes to represent ethnic- and gender-based humor, without introducing content differences that are incidental to the categorical differences. The content differences between the exemplary messages representing different types cannot be entirely eliminated, and even partial control over content differences is likely to have side effects that are worse than the original problem. The process of forcing equivalent content into categories of the sort that we are concerned with changes the conceptualization of the category and, in effect, changes the research question. For example, we might try to "equate" two jokes by using the same basic content, just varying a phrase or two to refer to ethnic- or gender-specific targets. But then the comparison is no longer between jokes playing on ethnic stereotypes and jokes playing on gender stereotypes, for these stereotypes do not underwrite the same punch-lines. Only the sort of joke that can take *any* malignable group as its butt can be used as a basis for the comparison, and this is no basis for inferences about the two classes of jokes as originally conceived.

When the research question calls for comparison between two classes of messages, the problem is how we can separate the differences between two *classes* from the differences among any two individual *examples*. That problem cannot be solved through artful choice of single examples.

Case–category confounding may occur in less obvious guises. For example, suppose we wish to know whether an advertisement will be more effective if placed near the beginning of a television program or near the end. The standard design, adapted for this question, would involve presentation of the advertisement to two audiences of the same program, with one audience getting the advertisement within the first five minutes and the other audience getting the advertisement within the last five minutes. The effect might be measured in terms of recall or other response variable. Now the use of a single advertisement may or may not be problematic, but the use of a single program as the context for the advertisement presents the same sort of problem as the use of a single joke to represent each of our two classes of jokes or the use of a single public service message to represent each of our two classes of appeals. Why?

Even if the two presentations of the advertisement turn out to be differentially effective, we can draw no valid categorical conclusion about placement at the beginning or end of the program. The reason is as before: The categorical difference (beginning/end) is only one of many differences between the two segments in which the ad could occur, and although one of two concrete placements is demonstrably better than the other, we have no way of knowing whether this is because of the beginning/end contrast or one of the other differences between the segments. Again, the variation in the categorical variable of interest is confounded with other variations, so that categorical interpretation is unjustified.

Designs in which a single message is observed as an example of each message category of interest do not normally permit any sort of categorical conclusion, because they permit no separation of categorical features and idiosyncratic features of individual cases. Although a comparison between two concrete messages can certainly tell us which of these two concrete messages is more effective or more comprehensible or more memorable, the comparison offers no warrant for any particular categorical account of the difference. The vulnerability of a conclusion to case–category confounding can be judged in any particular case by considering whether it is possible that the difference attributed to the distinction of interest might in fact be attributed to some other distinction among the concrete messages compared.

Figure 2.2 offers an abstract representation of the categorical comparison problem. We are interested in comparing two categories (altruistic appeals and self-interest appeals, or gender-based jokes and ethnic-based jokes). The members of these categories vary, even within categories, in their effects on the dependent variable. We can think

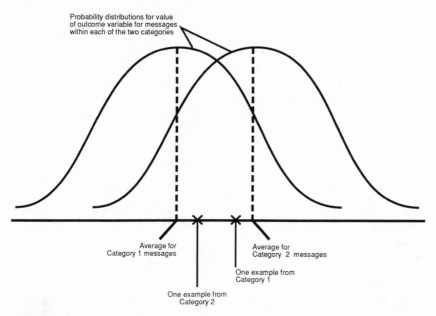

Probability distributions for value
of outcome variable for messages
within each of the two categories

Average for
Category 1 messages

Average for
Category 2 messages

One example from
Category 1

One example from
Category 2

FIGURE 2.2. How the relationship between case and category affects our ability to compare categories.

of a distribution of persuasiveness levels within each category of appeal, or a distribution of offensiveness levels within each category of joke, and it is not the level of the response variable associated with the individual message, but the average or expected level of the response variable across a category that is of interest to us. The choice of one member from one category and one member from the other category is always inadequate as a basis for comparing the categories because we have no way of judging the position of the case with respect to other cases within the same category. Notice that the *apparent* difference between gender-based jokes and ethnic-based jokes is entirely dependent on which particular jokes we choose to make the comparison. So, for example, if we choose an unusually offensive ethnic joke and compare it with a strictly average gender-based joke, we may be tempted to conclude that ethnic jokes are more offensive when in fact they are, on the average, less offensive. This is the source of the weaknesses in the unreplicated categorical comparison.

Now if you are thinking ahead, you'll realize that any comparison between two categories of objects will depend on the cases selected to represent the categories, and that any effort to compare, say, ethnic jokes and gender jokes could be very misleading if the examples are unrepresentative. In Chapter 3 I will recommend an alternative design that is intended to avoid case–category confounding, and then it will be necessary to show that my alternative is not vulnerable to the same threats as is the unreplicated categorical comparison. The threats that afflict the unreplicated categorical comparison are avoidable, but it is too soon to begin that discussion.

Concealed Insufficiency of Data

When attempting to make generic claims about a category of objects, it is normally necessary to examine more than one member of the category, and this is increasingly so as the within-category diversity increases. Drawing conclusions about a category based on only one or only a few cases is a familiar error in reasoning often labeled "hasty generalization." In message experiments, errors of this type are concealed by an appearance of multiplicity. Specifically, one message may yield any number of "observations" in the form of responses registered by many human respondents. The status of the message as a single "case" is disguised by the otherwise familiar structure of the data-set, which encourages treatment of each respondent as having contributed an independent observation.

Consider again the designs sketched in Figure 2.1. Let's say we divide 200 subjects into two independent groups, presenting one group with the first of our experimental messages and the other group with the second experimental message. The comparison between the two *messages* involves 200 independent observations. The comparison between the two *categories* involves only two independent observations: the aggregate response to one message representing the first category and the aggregate response to one message representing the other category. The insufficiency of the data to support categorical comparisons is concealed by the appearance of having many observations per cell.

The problem of concealed insufficiency is particularly likely to arise in designs incorporating several message variables, so that there are a relatively large number of "cells" to be represented by individual messages. Suppose we have three different independent variables to be considered simultaneously: basis for humor (ethnic stereotype vs. gender stereotype), form of joke (question–answer vs. narrative), and length (short vs. long). To have one joke of each type, we would need eight jokes altogether, so the contrast between ethnic-based jokes and gender-based jokes would be made on four jokes of each type.

When the design is made more complex in this way, the insufficiency of the data to support categorical claims may be more difficult to spot, but it is still problematic. Suppose, again, that we divide our 200 respondents into groups of equal size; this time we will have 25 people to rate each joke for offensiveness. For each main effect comparison (between ethnic-based and gender-based jokes or between question–answer and narrative jokes or between short and long jokes), we have a total of 200 individual ratings, but still only eight independent observations—four jokes within each of two types. This is, of course, much better than *one* joke within each type, but it still smacks of hasty generalization.

Notice, too, that the inclusion of eight jokes within the design assures four messages per type *only* for the main effect comparisons. Any effort to analyze interactions or simple effects will involve fewer examples per type. For example, the three-way interaction of basis for humor, form of joke, and length is dependent on a single case per cell, so that, for example, a single unusually offensive joke among the eight could lead to the appearance of a three-way interaction. Likewise, if we choose to look at the simple main effects of basis for humor at each of the two levels of form, we end up comparing, within each level of form, two gender-based jokes with two ethnic-based jokes. Notice that in this design, the sufficiency of the data declines with the specificity of the analysis, but even at its best the design offers what would appear to be a poor basis for categorical comparison.

If we wish to make claims about the relative offensiveness of ethnic jokes and gender jokes, it is more important to know how many jokes of each type were examined, and the question of how many people were observed as registers of the effect is strictly secondary. This common-sensical premise should be reflected in the characteristics of our statistical analyses, but in standard research practice, it is not. Within the unreplicated categorical comparison design, no matter how complex, the comparisons made among message types are sensitive to the number of human respondents observed, but not to the number of message cases.

If our hypothetical experiment should produce a statistically significant main effect for basis of humor—that is, a significant difference between the gender jokes and the ethnic jokes—we would remain poorly positioned to make any claim about the relative offensiveness of the two types of jokes. An obvious limitation of the evidence is that it involves a small number of cases, and is therefore vulnerable to all the dangers associated with hasty generalization. The "significance" of the finding might seem to assure that the generalization is *not* hasty, but this is not so, for the test is quite insensitive to the number of messages involved, and indeed, insensitive to the effect of the message *examples* on the estimate of the categorical effect. This topic will receive much more detailed attention in Chapter 3. But to anticipate that discussion, the significance of the main effect can be taken only as evidence that two concrete groups of jokes differ in their average offensiveness, not as evidence that two abstract *types* of jokes differ in their average offensiveness. The usual sort of significance test done in an experiment of this kind does not respond at all to the burden of proof involved in documenting a claim about message effects.

Think about this: If the eight jokes, considered simply as individual messages, differ significantly from one another in offensiveness, then it is guaranteed that some "effect" within the design will turn up significant as well. This is a consequence of the confounding of the individual cases with the categories, and it cannot be escaped without a fundamental change in design-and-analysis strategies. A concealed insufficiency of data is particularly likely to occur in an experiment like this one, where multiple independent variables lead to the use of a relatively large number of individual messages, but where the statistical testing fails to disentangle the effects of individual messages from the effects of message categories.

This issue has statistical implications too complicated to be discussed at this point, but we will return to it in Chapter 3, then again in Chapter 5. What is important for the present purpose is to see that questions about the sufficiency of a set of observations to support a comparison of message categories should be answered first in terms of the number of messages observed, and not in terms of the number of people observed. A rough and ready test for sufficiency can be formulated as follows: Considering only the number of messages observed in an experiment as individual cases, does the categorical claim drawn from the experiment appear to be an example of hasty generalization? If so, the number of human subjects observed is entirely irrelevant to the insufficiency of the data to support the claim. And regrettably, for vast numbers of message experiments, the categorical conclusions drawn from the experiments do indeed appear to be hasty generalizations.

UNREPLICATED TREATMENT COMPARISONS

Much of what is currently believed about strategic message variation derives from studies in which the strategy variable is itself manipulated within a message and evaluated in terms of audience response. There is nothing wrong with this, in principle, but the standard design evaluates the effect of the manipulation within a single illustrative message, and there is something wrong with this. The treatment is unreplicated across messages, and this blocks inference about the effect of the treatment in the same way that an unreplicated categorical comparison blocks inference about the differences between the categories.

The basic structure of the unreplicated treatment comparison is shown in Figure 2.3. The difference between this design and the unreplicated categorical comparison is that it uses a single basic message, varied in some limited way to produce two or more versions. Following Hunter, Hamilton and Allen (1989), I will refer to this basic message as the "kernel" message. The experimentally manipulated versions of the kernel message will usually be presented to independent groups of respondents, though repeated-measures designs can certainly be imagined within this general framework.

A very typical application of the unreplicated treatment comparison design would be in any of the dozens of experiments on the effect of fear appeals in persuasion. The underlying issue is whether audiences are more likely to be swayed by extremely fearful materials than by more moderate appeals. The standard design is to select a basic per-

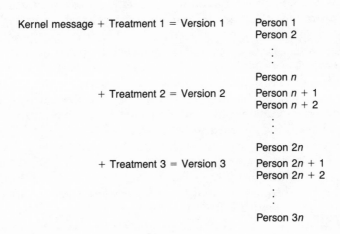

FIGURE 2.3. Unreplicated treatment comparison design. n = the number of people per cell.

suasive message and, within the context of its main claims, to vary the level of threat offered as motivation for compliance. The precedent for this line of work is found in a study reported by Janis and Feshbach (1953); many dozens of studies have repeated the basic procedures, in most cases using a single message as the context for the manipulation of fear. In the Janis and Feshbach study, the kernel message was a lecture on the importance of dental hygiene, and the variation in fear was contained in what was claimed—and shown—about the consequences of poor dental hygiene. Other studies have been similar in their approaches to manipulation of fear, using either variations in the verbal content or variations in accompanying visual materials or some combination of both. But the common feature in nearly all studies has been the use of a single kernel message to which the fear manipulation is applied to produce contrasting versions.

Now, as before, any one of these experiments can be understood at two quite different levels: as evaluating several alternative versions of a single particular message (in order, say, to decide which one to use as a nationwide teaching device), or, on the other hand, as evaluating a generic effect (in order to test a theoretical hypothesis or to underwrite practical advice). Interpretations at the first level pose few problems; interpretations at the second level pose problems insurmountable at the level of individual studies conducted using the standard design. The reasons are complex, but can be exemplified in a preliminary way in terms of a criticism against Janis and Feshbach that has been circulating informally for some time: Their conclusion that high-fear appeals are less effective than low-fear appeals has been challenged on the grounds that the concrete appeal chosen to evoke high fear also—unintendedly—strained credulity. The low-fear appeal mentioned familiar consequences of poor dental hygiene such as cavities and tooth decay, while the high-fear appeal asserted a link between poor dental hygiene and life-threatening diseases, such as "arthritic paralysis, kidney damage, or total blindness." Even if accepted as genuine, the link between dental hygiene and these health problems would have to be assumed to be weak.[1]

The challenge to Janis and Feshbach's conclusions points to a general weakness in unreplicated treatment comparisons. The weakness follows from the possibility that the introduction of one dimension of difference through manipulation of a message element might carry with it an unintended differentiation along another dimension. This possibility makes for ambiguity in identification of cause. But despite a wide recognition of the problems in the Janis and Feshbach study, researchers have persisted in mimicking its design, each one supplying a new single-case comparison or (worse) repeating a single-case comparison using the kernel message from an earlier study.

As should be clear from this initial example, the standard treatment comparison design suffers from extremely fundamental weaknesses. These weaknesses stem from the use of messages as bases for the operationalization of message variables or, more properly, from the belief that individual messages embody the contrasts of interest in a direct, straightforward way. Like the unreplicated categorical comparison design, the unreplicated treatment comparison design is afflicted by a number of identifiable threats to validity. Each of these threats follows from the fact that the conclusion drawn is generic and the evidence presented is case-specific. We will consider three general threats to the validity of conclusions drawn from unreplicated treatment comparisons: *superfluous variation*, *"gestalt" effects*, and *unexamined variability in treatment effect*.

Superfluous Variation

A conclusion is threatened by what I call *superfluous variation* if the research procedures used to create one sort of distinction bring about other unintended distinctions. The label "superfluous" is meant to indicate that differences other than those defined by the independent variable of interest have been introduced. This is, of course, a variant of confounding, and it can occur in a wide range of research situations other than experiments on message variables. Ordinarily, superfluous variation appears as a failure of "experimental control," a failure, that is, to equate conditions across the levels of the treatment variable. Steps taken to equate materials and conditions are aimed at eliminating superfluous variation.

Within the context of message effects research, superfluous variation threatens conclusions about the effect of a treatment in many experiments in which the treatment is applied to a single kernel message. Superficially, it might appear that applying a given experimental manipulation to a single "controlled" kernel is a direct response to the superfluous variation threat, in that the controlled kernel equates message features other than the one manipulated. But this appearance is false. Rarely, if ever, is it possible to "control" variables other than the one we wish to manipulate, even when the kernel message is kept constant across treatments.

One version of this problem appeared in the Janis and Feshbach study of the effect of fear appeals, discussed above. In that experiment, the manipulation of fear was implemented through variations in lecture content that must also be assumed to have introduced other differences. Other examples of the problem could be found throughout the literature on persuasive message effects. Refer back to Figure 2.3. Whatever is added to the kernel to produce the contrasting versions may involve manipulations not only of the intended independent variable, but also of other, unintended variables. Differences in outcome are not attributable to any one influence, as can be seen in Figure 2.4.

I would like to emphasize that generic conclusions about a treatment variable justified in terms of a difference between one matched pair of messages are threatened (but not necessarily refuted) by a charge of superfluous variation. Superfluous variation is, in principle, a rival hypothesis to any claim about the source of the difference, just as "history" and "maturation" are, in principle, rival hypotheses to claims about treatment effects based on experiments without control groups. In practice, any rival hypothesis may itself be contested in terms of its specific relevance to the claim or in terms of its practical plausibility. Particular circumstances can always be invoked to argue that an in-principle threat does not in fact cast serious doubt on the conclusion. If, for example, the treatment variable is "extratextual" rather than "intratextual," one may be able to build quite a good case that there has been no superfluous variation within the message. This would be the case for messages subjected to such things as context manipulations or source manipulations, insofar as the manipulations of context and source are not themselves vulnerable to case–category confounding

Kernel + Treatment 1
     Low fear
     Familiar content
     Believable content
     Short-term threat
     Etc.
  + Treatment 2
     Medium fear
     Unfamiliar content
     Unbelievable content
     Intermediate-term threat
     Etc.
  + Treatment 3
     High fear
     Unfamiliar content
     Unbelievable content
     Long-term threat
     Etc.

FIGURE 2.4. The treatment as a source of superfluous variation.

or superfluous variation. However, even when it is possible to deflect a charge of superfluous variation in the messages, unreplicated treatment comparisons may be vulnerable to one or both of the two remaining threats.

"Gestalt" Effects

Manipulation of an independent variable within the context of a single controlled base message is vulnerable to another class of problems which I will term *"gestalt" effects*. By gestalt" effects I mean effects of a manipulated element on a surrounding "fixed" context. The presumption behind the standard unreplicated treatment comparison is that elements of a message can be isolated and subjected to treatment, leaving the unmanipulated portions of the message unchanged. This would be reasonable if message meaning and message effects were simple cumulations of the meanings and effects of all the elements within the message, but there are good reasons for doubting whether this is so.

Consider the following brief descriptions of a hypothetical person (drawn from a study of impression formation conducted by Delia, 1976).

Description 1: *Intelligent, clean,* efficient, level-headed, punctual, neat, ambitious, and self-disciplined.
Description 2: *Easy-going, sensitive,* efficient, level-headed, punctual, neat, ambitious, and self-disciplined.

Notice that each of the two descriptions contains eight trait-attributions, and that six of these are "held constant" across lists. The contrast between the two lists would seem to be isolated to two trait pairs: "intelligent and clean" versus "easy-going and sensitive." Now, it happens that these two trait lists result in markedly different estimates of how likable and how socially attractive the person described would be; the second list produced the more favorable ratings in Delia's study. We might like to suppose that the difference in likability and social attractiveness is a simple matter of preference for "easy-going and sensitive" people over "intelligent and clean" people. But as Delia's study established, this simple hypothesis is untenable, for, in isolation, the traits "intelligent" and "clean" were the most positive elements in the trait lists, so it is hard to see how substituting them for "easy-going" and "sensitive" could *worsen* the impression formed. Moreover, the evaluative ratings people gave for the six traits "held constant" changed depending on whether the lists were headed by one pair or the other: Each of the six traits, in fact, was evaluated more positively within the context of the second list than within the context of the first. The difference between the two lists is not reducible to a difference between the two substituted pairs of traits.

Delia's study was not designed primarily to make a methodological point, but to make a substantive point about impression formation. But notice that what it shows about the role of information in impression formation has important implications for what we think about messages and message components, and therefore for what we think about our ability to isolate and manipulate individual message features. Delia's study demonstrates that people do not interpret elements within even very simple messages one at a time and then add these interpretations together to arrive at an overall response. The relationship between message and message element is likely to be more complex than that.

What might gestalt effects of this sort look like within the context of an experiment on persuasive message effects? Consider the many ways in which manipulation of one message element might affect other individual elements apparently held constant. In the manipulation of language intensity, the use of very strong adjectives and adverbs at selected points may create a baseline against which other (non-manipulated) elements are judged. Suppose both the intense and non-intense versions of a message conclude by characterizing a proposal as "unwise" and by urging that it be "opposed." Whether "unwise" and "oppose" will have the same meaning and the same impact in both messages is an open question. Within the context of the intense message this ending may appear very weak, while within the context of the nonintense message it may appear quite strong. Then the intensity manipulation has introduced not one, but two differentiations between the two messages being compared: the intended differentiation in overall levels of language intensity and an unintended differentiation in some quality of organization we might call "direction of flow" (extreme-to-moderate vs. moderate-to-extreme) or some quality of conclusion strength captured in the contrast between understatement and overstatement.

Now it happens that only some small subset of experimental manipulations occurring within unreplicated treatment comparisons involve replacements of isolated words in a fashion similar to replacement of traits in a list or replacement of isolated adjectives and adverbs in an essay. But the implication of Delia's results is very general, for we must assume that if simple word substitutions within a "fixed" context alter the meaning of the context as a whole, then substitutions of sentences and whole paragraphs will have even more marked effects on context.

Consider how the manipulation of larger (and more typical) message elements might alter the overall quality of a message in some important way. For example, the manipulation of argument-sidedness, normally accomplished by adding refutational arguments to initially one-sided presentations, might change the overall organization, coherence, or flow of the message. (There is nothing about the concept of two-sidedness that makes this necessary: Two-sidedness is not a matter of arguing both sides of a question, but a matter of recognizing and responding to potential objections.) Then the insertion of the two-sided material produces two versions of the message that differ in more than one respect: in two-sidedness and in, say, overall coherence.

To say that single-message designs are vulnerable to gestalt effects is not, of course, to say that gestalt effects always occur, nor is it to say that when they do occur they always constitute a plausible rival hypothesis to claims about the effects of the treatment variable. As with any abstract category of rival hypotheses, the particular claim being made or the particular local circumstances may disarm gestalt effects as a substantive counterclaim. Within the limits of a single-message experiment, there is no principled solution to the threat of gestalt effects, but only case-specific reasons for believing the threat to be unrealized. If possible, we would like to have design and analysis strategies that work whether or not the manipulation of the independent variable has the capacity to introduce other version-to-version differences, directly through superfluous variations, or indirectly through gestalt effects.

Unexamined Variability in Treatment Effects

Designs in which an experimental manipulation is applied to a single controlled message suffer from yet another threat that I will term *unexamined variability in treatment effects*. An interest in the relative effectiveness of one-sided and two-sided argument or in the relative effectiveness of promises and threats implies some sort of domain of applicability: perhaps a domain as broad as all persuasive messages or all interpersonal compliance-gaining situations. Now nothing in the research question itself or in any substantive body of knowledge we have about communication would justify a belief that effects of these sort are uniform throughout their domains. Indeed, common experience suggests that whatever the general advantage of two-sidedness over one-sidedness or of promise over threat, there will be exceptional cases in which the general effect reverses and many more ordinary cases in which the general effect fluctuates in magnitude. Where this is so, a treatment effect observed for a single manipulated message is always inescapably ambiguous.

Concretely, we might imagine "the advantage of two-sidedness over one-sidedness" as a variable in its own right with a value or range of values for any given kernel message. These values might have an identifiable central tendency (some positive number if two-sidedness is generally advantageous and some negative number if it is generally disadvantageous), but the values for individual messages would spread around the average value. Figure 2.5 portrays a domain of messages as varying in their "susceptibility" to variations in the independent variable of interest. The horizontal axis represents possible treatment effects for individual messages; positive values represent, say, an advantage of Treatment A over Treatment B for any given message, and negative values represent an advantage of Treatment B

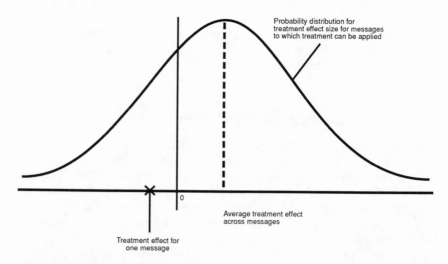

FIGURE 2.5. How variability in the effect of the treatment from message to message affects our ability to estimate the "average" treatment effect.

over Treatment A. The vertical axis is tied to frequency or probability, and the mean of the distribution might be thought of as the "average" or "expected" advantage of Treatment A over Treatment B. In an experiment applying the treatment to a single message, there is no way to tell how the message observed relates to the distribution of the treatment effect throughout the domain of interest. We may have selected for study a message particularly hospitable to two-sidedness or a message exceptionally inhospitable to two-sidedness.[2] The result is that a treatment effect measured for the concrete message at hand is uninterpretable in any general sense: We know only that the particular two-sided message studied is better (or worse) than its particular one-sided partner, and nothing at all at a general level about two-sidedness.

Unless the treatment effect of interest can be assumed or shown to be entirely uniform from one application to another, general conclusions can never be justifiably drawn from measurements taken on any one application. In the language of analysis of variance, if a treatment "interacts" with its context—which is just to say that its direction or size differ from one context to another—a single message experiment confounds the main effect of the treatment with the treatment-by-message interaction effect. The error can be avoided only by examining the variability of the treatment effect from one message to another, hence the label given to this threat. The problem of unexamined variability invites a solution based partly on design and partly on statistical analysis, and thus we will return to it later. However, the inferential problem should not be misunderstood: The defect in single-message experiments is not that they try to draw conclusions about effects that are themselves variable, but that they do so without attempting to measure or describe that variability. Meaningful conclusions can certainly be drawn about effects that are nonuniform, but they cannot be justified without data on the nature and extent of the nonuniformity.

SUMMARY AND IMPLICATIONS

In this chapter we have analyzed two standard designs used in experiments on message variables, both involving a test of a general hypothesis based on observation of a single message-to-message contrast. Whether aimed at comparison among message categories or evaluation of treatment effects, designs based on only one message per experimental condition are plagued by threats to validity. For unreplicated categorical comparisons, the two most fundamental threats to any categorical conclusion are case–category confounding and concealed insufficiency of data. For unreplicated treatment comparisons, there are three serious threats: superfluous variation introduced by the treatment, "gestalt" effects, and unexamined case-to-case variability in the treatment effect.

These threats are not proposed as an exhaustive list of the problems plaguing single-message designs, but they are offered as a set of handles for getting hold of some slippery problems. All of these threats identify substantive rival hypotheses to claims put forward routinely in the research literature on communication processes and effects. As I have tried to emphasize in the development of the particular threats and to illustrate by way of examples, not every experiment structured in such a way as to suggest vulnerability on one point or another will result in an invalid claim. In this respect, the threats to validity described here are similar to those inventoried by Campbell and Stanley (1963); they are challenges, not refutations, and the seriousness of the challenge is always relative to particular local circumstances.

What stance should be taken toward single-message designs, given this list of potential problems, any of which might be disarmed by the local particulars? Let's consider an analogy, drawn from Campbell and Stanley's familiar list. It is widely recognized that certain kinds of conclusions are weakly supported, if they are supported at all, by certain arrangements of data. For example, if we test a group of people twice, administering a treatment before the second measurement, and infer treatment effects from the difference between the two measurements, the inference is vulnerable to a rival hypothesis normally labeled "testing effects." The design solution is to use a control group given both tests but no treatment, so as to be able to "correct" for the effect of testing. But even in the absence of a control group it is sometimes possible to disarm testing effects as a rival hypothesis. If the test is one that cannot reasonably be thought to change the person tested, then differences from first to second measurement cannot be attributed to the test. Testing would not be a strong rival hypothesis if the measurements were unobtrusive, for example. But the possibility of using local particulars to defeat a rival hypothesis in some particular case should never be mistaken for a general defense of a weak design. The fact that testing does not threaten *every* study of this type does not diminish its force as an *issue* to be taken into account.

The rival hypotheses I have identified stand as a general critique of single-message designs in the same way that Campbell and Stanley's rival hypotheses stand as general critiques of nonrandomized experiments and experiments without relevant comparison groups. Although the application of any particular threat within any particular study is not automatic, it should be clear that these threats identify serious structural weaknesses in the standard designs and that these serious structural weaknesses give rise to serious logical errors when generic conclusions are drawn. In the next chapter, I will propose some alternative design prototypes that incorporate structural solutions to these structural problems.

THREE

Replicated Categorical Comparisons

As we saw in Chapter 2, unreplicated designs suffer from serious threats to validity. These threats are direct consequences of a failure to incorporate message replications. Although altering our observational strategies cannot change the nature of messages or the difficulties we encounter in our efforts to make generic statements about them, improvements in design can indeed change the nature of our evidence and the quality of our empirical arguments. Once we have become aware of the objections that can be raised against a class of claims, it is possible to devise strategies for answering these objections. So, for example, an awareness of how case–category confounding affects claims about the categories can prompt us to find evidence that categorical differences are *not* reducible to case differences.

In this chapter and the next, I will describe some design prototypes built on the model of the standard designs, but improved through addition of an explicit replications factor. Although for the most part these chapters simply elaborate suggestions made in earlier essays that my colleagues and I have published, this will nevertheless be the first systematic discussion of how these suggestions would work out in practice. Attached to a general development of the proposal will be extended discussion of how the use of message replications helps to answer the rival hypotheses inventoried in Chapter 2.

Chapters 3 and 4 present design and analysis suggestions for two distinct research situations, previewed in Chapter 2 as a rough differentiation between categorical comparisons and evaluations of treatment effects. This chapter will deal with design of experiments aimed at comparisons among message classes and Chapter 4 with experiments aimed at evaluating the effect of a treatment applied to messages. The extension of these discussions to more complicated research situations is quite straightforward and will simply be appended to Chapter 4.

The major basis for differentiation between the two research situations, as before, will be how we have conceptualized the independent variable: as a classification of messages or as a treatment applicable within messages. We encounter considerable complexity (and many opportunities for equivocation) in trying to draw this distinction within the context of message experiments. To begin with, as mentioned in Chapter 2, some variables can be conceptualized either as a classification or as a treatment, depending on the concrete particulars of the research question. Many classifications of persuasive appeals could be made to resemble treatments by embedding them within some "kernel" message built as a framework for the contrasting appeals. But additionally, a message variable can have a dual role within the experiment, as a classification (applied to individual messages) and as a treatment (administered to individual human respondents). For example, in evaluating the relative effectiveness of promise and threat, we would likely present each respondent with either a promise or a threat, taking the measured response as the dependent variable. The strategy variable may be seen in this context as a treatment given to respondents, but it is certainly not a treatment applied to messages, for any given message either is a promise or a threat or a member of some other category not presently relevant. For the purposes of this chapter and the next, the distinction between a classification variable and a treatment variable is a matter of the relationship between the values of the variable and the concrete messages studied, rather than of the relationship between the values of the variable and the individual human respondents observed. The first of our two basic research situations deals with message classifications in this sense, and the second deals with message treatments in this sense.

The basic design principle to be elaborated in this chapter and the next can be summed up as follows: *Wherever the standard designs use a single message, substitute multiple messages as replications.* To be sure, not every experiment will need multiple messages in order to make its case; this should be quite clear already. But every experiment using messages to represent a category or to instantiate a treatment should be scrutinized for vulnerability to the threats overviewed in Chapter 2, and where the use of a single message opens the interpretation of the experiment to serious rival hypotheses, multiple messages should be used.

DESIGN PROTOTYPES

A simple repair to the unreplicated categorical comparison is to add message replications within each category of interest. This design will be termed a *replicated categorical comparison*. Since messages are included as replications, they are assigned the same logical status as respondents. One implication of this is that they are normally treated as levels of a "random factor" in the statistical analysis.[1] To forestall a predictable objection, this design repair does not necessarily involve a large increase in the number of respondents, as explained later.

What does a replicated categorical comparison look like? Any number of actual experimental designs would be acceptable implementations of this proposal. The main differences among them arise from the relationship between the messages used as cases and the human respondents used as registers of the effect. A replicated categorical comparison always involves direct or indirect nesting of messages within message categories, but several variations are possible. The basic defining features of the replicated categorical comparison are shown in Figure 3.1. The design differs from the unreplicated categorical comparison in incorporation of several different messages within each category; the messages chosen for each category represent independent

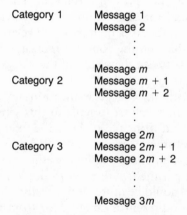

Category 1	Message 1
	Message 2
	⋮
	Message m
Category 2	Message m + 1
	Message m + 2
	⋮
	Message $2m$
Category 3	Message $2m$ + 1
	Message $2m$ + 2
	⋮
	Message $3m$

FIGURE 3.1. The replicated categorical comparison design. Note: m = the number of messages per message category.

"samples." Instead of having all respondents within a treatment level respond to the same message, the available respondents are divided among the message replications.

Now, the purpose of adding the replications is to respond to the arguments that can be raised against unreplicated categorical comparisons. The confounding of category differences with case-to-case differences—a fundamental barrier to categorical interpretation of single-case comparisons—is not in fact eliminated within the replicated design. The average response to messages within each category examined will be dependent, to some degree, on what particular messages are chosen to represent each category. The replicated design responds to the problem of case–category confounding, not by eliminating the confounding, but by providing a way of taking it into account. Specifically, the messages within each category are used argumentatively as a basis for projecting the amount of category-to-category difference that would be expected based on case-to-case variations alone. This is the point of treating the message replication factor as "random." Notice that case–category confounding refers not to an objective circumstance, but to an objection that can be raised against certain empirical arguments and answered by others. Category differences still "contain" case-specific differences, even in the replicated design, but because the replicated design also allows an independent estimate of these case-specific differences, the confounding is only partial, and its effect on the comparison can be evaluated statistically.

To extend an example from Chapter 2, our experiment on ethnic-based and gender-based humor could be redesigned to include, say, 20 different jokes of each type. We would be comparing not one ethnic joke with one gender joke, but average offensiveness ratings of 20 ethnic jokes and 20 gender jokes. The statistical analysis would recognize "jokes within categories" as a source of random variation in the estimates of the category means, so that differences in offensiveness from one *category* to another would be taken as evidence for a categorical effect only if they exceeded the sort of differences expectable from joke-to-joke variation alone.

This description is, at this point, too abstract to fit actual research circumstances. Figure 3.1 shows the relationship between the unreplicated and replicated categorical comparison designs, but does not show how replicated categorical comparisons would actually appear in research. In particular, while the relationship between individual messages and message categories is displayed, the relationships among categories, messages, and respondents are not. There are many variations on the replicated categorical comparison.

Consider first a straightforward single-factor independent-groups design. There is one independent variable of interest (with, for simplicity, two levels), and there are two replication factors (messages and people) arranged hierarchically as shown in Figure 3.2. As in Figure 3.1, the messages "nested" under each category are not paired in any way across categories, but are entirely independent cases of their respective categories. The same is true of persons; each person appears in the design only once, as the recipient of one particular message within one particular category.

Statistically, there are three separable sources of variance in the design, the classification variable C, the messages replication factor

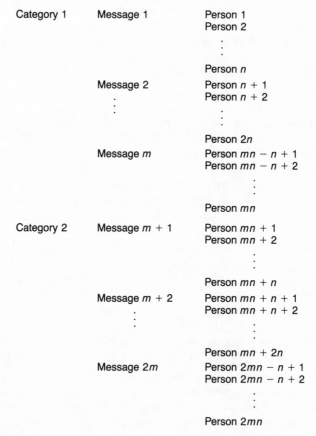

FIGURE 3.2. A categorical comparison with respondents nested within messages. Note: m = the number of messages per category; n = the number of respondents per message.

M, and the respondents factor P. Both replications factors (messages and people) are considered random, and the central objective is to test the differences between the classifications. Appropriate statistical tests can be found in any comprehensive treatment of the analysis of variance (e.g., Keppel, 1982; Winer, 1971), and also in the literature dealing with analysis of language experiments following from Coleman (1964) and Clark (1973). Some basic concepts pertinent to choice of tests are reviewed in the Appendix, where several illustrative designs are discussed in detail. For this particular design, the F test for testing the null hypothesis that the classes do not differ on the dependent variable is a ratio of the mean squares for category and for messages within category, that is:

$$F = MS_C/MS_{M/C}, \; df = c - 1, \; c(m - 1)$$

where c is the number of classes and m is the number of message replications per class.

An alternative design, appropriate when messages are easier to come by than respondents, is to form independent groups of respondents assigned to classifications and to present each respondent with his or her own unique message set. The design remains hierarchical, with one replication factor nested within the other, except that now the messages factor is nested within the respondents factor rather than the reverse. This arrangement is shown in Figure 3.3. The F test for the difference between classes is correspondingly altered; now the ratio is between the mean squares for class and for persons within classes, as shown in the Appendix under Design 2:

$$F = MS_C/MS_{P/C}, \; df = c - 1, \; c(n - 1)$$

where c is again the number of classes and n is the number of respondents per class.

But this does not mean that the test of category differences ignores case variations, since the respondents variance now "contains" variance due to cases, just as in the previous design, the messages variance contained variance due to human respondents (see Appendix). The choice of whether to nest persons within messages or messages within persons can depend entirely on which the researcher has more of.[2]

If each respondent gets a unique message, so that there is a one-to-one correspondence of messages and respondents, the two replication factors reduce to one (Coleman, 1964). In Figure 3.4, the index numbers attached to each respondent/message pair are unique, and the only

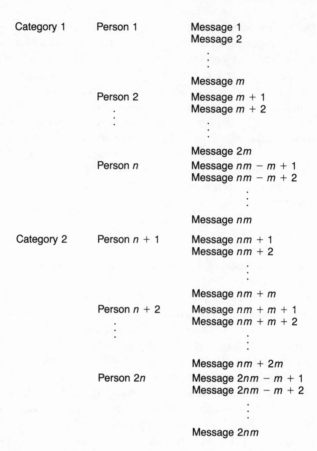

FIGURE 3.3. A categorical comparison with messages nested within persons. Note: m = the number of messages given to each person; n = the number of persons assigned to each category.

possible error term for testing class effects is the replications-within-classes mean square.

For some research situations, it will be convenient to abandon the hierarchical arrangements described above in favor of multiple-response designs. The reasons for choosing a design of this sort are similar to those for choosing a repeated-measures design: to increase the number of observations within a fixed number of respondents, and to decrease the "error variance." Many complicated arrangements are possible; we will consider two, one of which involves both the classification variable and the messages as repeated factors and the other of which involves only the messages within classes as a repeated factor.

With certain kinds of experimental messages, it is reasonable to ask respondents to respond to each and every message in the experiment (Coleman, 1964). For example, to return to our hypothetical experiment comparing the offensiveness of ethnic-based and gender-based jokes, we might well locate 20 examples of each type and have every respondent in the experiment rate the offensiveness of all 40. (Quite obviously, this would be an unsuitable arrangement if the messages being studied were long or demanding, as for example, essays or speeches.) In this design, the respondents factor is said to be "crossed" with both messages and classes. In Figure 3.5, it should be noticed that the same n respondents are observed repeatedly, responding to each and every message in the design.

Finding an appropriate F test for testing the class differences is complicated, because neither of the two random factors "contains" the other; that is, persons are not nested under messages, and messages are not nested under persons. In psycholinguistics, where designs of this type commonly appear in experiments using words and sentences, the usual solution is to construct a "quasi F test," a ratio formed of some composite of mean squares in both the numerator and denominator. Generally, one constructs such a test by examining the expected mean squares for every effect in the design and searching for combinations of terms such that the composite in the numerator differs from the composite in the denominator only by a variance component representing the effect to be tested. General methods for finding expected

Category 1	Person 1/Message 1
	Person 2/Message 2
	.
	.
	.
	Person r/Message r
Category 2	Person r + 1/Message r + 1
	Person r + 2/Message r + 2
	.
	.
	.
	Person $2r$/Message $2r$

FIGURE 3.4. A categorical comparison with a single replication factor. Note: r = the number of observations in each cell; each observation represents the pairing of one person with one message, and neither person nor message appears more than once.

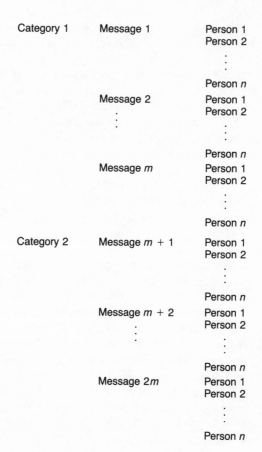

Category 1	Message 1	Person 1
		Person 2
		⋮
		Person n
	Message 2	Person 1
		Person 2
	⋮	⋮
		Person n
	Message m	Person 1
		Person 2
		⋮
		Person n
Category 2	Message m + 1	Person 1
		Person 2
		⋮
		Person n
	Message m + 2	Person 1
		Person 2
	⋮	⋮
		Person n
	Message 2m	Person 1
		Person 2
		⋮
		Person n

FIGURE 3.5. Multiple response design I: Respondents crossed with class. Note: m = the number of messages per message category; n = the number of persons responding to each message.

mean squares for any design are widely available (e.g., in Glass & Hopkins, 1984; Keppel, 1982; or Winer, 1971). For the design we are considering (treated in the Appendix as Design 3), the class differences can be tested by forming a ratio of two sums of mean squares proposed by Clark (1973).

$$F' = (MS_C + MS_{P \times M/C})/(MS_{M/C} + MS_{P \times C})$$

Degrees of freedom for this F' ratio must be approximated. General methods for doing so can be found in Winer (1971, pp. 377–378), but for this particular F' ratio, the degrees of freedom for both numerator and denominator may be obtained by rounding off to an integer value a function of the component mean squares and their corresponding degrees of freedom. Notice that both numerator and denominator are composed as the sum of two mean squares. If we denote the value of these two mean squares in each case as u and v, the degrees of freedom are obtained by computing the following ratio, once for the numerator and once for the denominator, rounding off the result to the nearest integer value in each case.

$$df = [(u + v)^2]/[(u^2/df_u) + (v^2/df_v)]$$

The application of quasi F ratios of this sort to experiments using language replications was proposed by Clark (1973), and since the publication of that essay, the distribution of some typical instantiations of the quasi F ratio have been extensively researched.[3] Unfortunately, standard analysis of variance computer programs are not well-adapted to problems of this kind, and test statistics may have to be computed by hand. However, sums of squares and mean squares generated by computer can be used as the basis for these computations, so that the actual hand computation can be limited to adding and dividing a few numbers.

If respondents cannot, for some reason, be presented with messages from both classes, it is still possible to present each respondent with all of the messages within a class. Figure 3.6 displays this design. This would be a reasonable choice if the classes were such that items within one class might affect interpretation of items within the other class. For example, if we wished to have respondents rate the vividness of literal and metaphoric descriptions of objects, the appearance of metaphoric descriptions in the list might prompt subjects to interpret the literal descriptions as metaphorical as well. In such a case, it would be better to restrict respondents to one class of descriptions or the other, though no harm would be done by exposing respondents to multiple descriptions within a class.

Like the previous design, this one results in some statistical complexities as the cost of its greater efficiency in use of respondents. Expected mean squares for each effect in the design are given in the Appendix, under Design 4, and a quasi F ratio appropriate for testing the class difference can obviously be constructed as follows, with degrees of freedom generated as before:

$$F' = (MS_C + MS_{P \times M/C})/(MS_{P/C} + MS_{M/C})$$

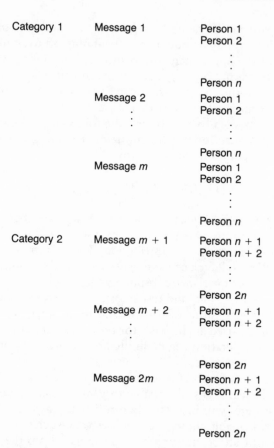

FIGURE 3.6. Multiple response design II. Respondents nested within class. Note: m = the number of messages per category; n = the number of respondents per message.

HOW REPLICATED DESIGNS RESPOND TO THREATS TO VALID INFERENCE

Recall the class of research questions for which we will want the replicated categorical comparison design: questions about differences in effects brought about by messages of several different, unrelated types. In trying to answer such questions, our primary task is to determine whether and how we can move from observation of several concrete messages to a generic claim about several message classes.

Examples of problems of this sort are comparisons among message types, comparisons among speech act types, comparisons among types of television programs, comparisons among types of interpersonal situations, and so on. These sorts of message variables are to individual messages what individual difference variables are to individual people. They are analogous, in other words, to variables like gender, race, and religion, that serve as bases for classifying people. We cannot experimentally manipulate these variables, for the nature of these variables is such that we cannot assign their values to any concrete case we choose to observe, but can only note what values the cases have.

As argued in Chapter 2, comparisons among several message types based on response to a single example of each type are so weak in principle as to be virtually worthless. The fundamental weakness of such designs flows from a confounding of category with case. Let us return for a moment to the concept of case–category confounding. The rival hypothesis invited by case–category confounding is some version of this: Variation observed among the experimental messages is not really related to the categorization of interest, but to some other incidental dimension of difference among the messages that we may think of as "case-specific." We may believe, or not, that case-specific variation flows from other identifiable variables; but as long as we believe that messages vary from one another in any respects other than the respect defined by our classification variable, this rival hypothesis is a threat to any categorical claim, and it must be answered by some sort of evidence that it is not true. We can consider both unreplicated and replicated designs for their ability to counter such threats.

Let us refer to the classification variable as C, and its levels as $C_1, C_2, \ldots, C_k$. In an unreplicated design, each level is represented by a single concrete message, $M_1, M_2, \ldots, M_k$. It should be plain by now that $M_1, M_2, \ldots$, are levels of a factor too, the "messages" factor, and that any one of these messages differs from the others not only in terms of its membership in one of the classes defined by C, but also in terms of other content dimensions that we will lump together under the label "case-specific features." The term case–category confounding should now have a perfectly concrete meaning. The levels of the classification variable—the categories to be compared— are completely confounded with the levels of the messages factor— the individual cases chosen to represent each category, with all the case-specific differences that that might imply. Anything that might be taken as evidence of category-to-category differences will be equally interpretable as mere case-to-case differences.

Relief from case–category confounding might be obtained in one of two ways: by getting an estimate of categorical differences that is independent of case-specific differences, or by getting an estimate of case-specific differences that is independent of categorical differences. The first of these two is usually impossible where message categories are concerned, for the messages that might be considered as members of any category will nearly always differ from one another in their effects on the dependent variable. The second approach requires only that we find a way to estimate case-specific differences, and that is easily accomplished within a replicated design.

Successfully addressing the problem of case–category confounding is a matter of ensuring that case-specific differences can be analytically separated from category differences. Observing multiple messages within each category is a straightforward solution. Within level C_1, we observe M_{11}, M_{12}, . . . , M_{1m}; within level C_2, we observe M_{21}, M_{22}, . . . , M_{2m}; and so on. The differences among the categories are now differences among averages, each computed over multiple cases; these differences continue to be confounded, in a certain sense, with case-specific differences, as noted above. We can think of the category means as differing partly as a function of genuine categorical differences and partly as a function of the individual messages used to estimate the category means. Alternatively, we can think of the variability between any two individual messages as representing a basic case-to-case difference, supplemented, or not, with a categorical difference, depending on whether the messages share a common categorization or differ in category; categorical differences, if any, can be considered metaphorically to be "piled on" over basic case-to-case differences. But the case-to-case differences can be estimated independently of the categorical differences, by evaluating the differences among messages *within* categories. The within-category variations offer an estimate of case-specific variation. Thus it becomes possible to partition the total variance among the individual messages into one part representing the combination of categorical differences and case-specific differences and another part representing the case differences. Having done so, we can compare the part representing categorical differences piled on case-specific differences with the part representing "pure" case-specific differences, so as to evaluate the hypothesis that apparent categorical differences are nothing more than what would be expected from case-specific differences within samples of a given size.

It is in this sense that replicated designs answer the charge of case–category confounding: In an unreplicated design, we cannot evaluate the possibility that ordinary, unsystematic differences between message and message will be mistaken for differences between category and category, while in a replicated design we can.

Now this does not solve all of our design problems, of course, nor does it guarantee freedom from other sorts of confounding (as has been pointed out by several critics of this proposal, including Morley, 1988, and Hunter et al., 1989). Other sorts of confounding may still afflict this design, and there is no mechanical way to preclude this possibility. Still, the replicated design is generally preferable to the unreplicated design in at least three respects: (1) in answering the "pure" case-category confounding objection considered above; (2) in weakening the case against other sorts of confounds involving unsuspected "other variables"; and (3) in creating the opportunity— absent within unreplicated designs—for nonstructural attacks on confounds involving these other variables.

Again we must return to an examination of the problem. Posit a purely hypothetical "other variable" X, whose levels X_1, X_2, . . . , X_k represent a competing way of categorizing the messages used to represent the levels of C—and hence, a rival hypothesis to the interpretation of differences among the messages as differences among the levels of C. A variable such as X can always be imagined, since there are no restrictions on what it may be like; it may even be a concatenation of levels of one variable (to compete with C_1 and C_2) and levels of another (to compete with C_3 through C_k). If we observe a number of threats and promises and find that the threats get better results than the promises, one may certainly challenge the conclusion that threats are more effective than promises by pointing to the fact, say, that the harms predicated by the threats used in the study are much more exaggerated than the benefits predicated by the promises used in the study. The contrast between threat and promise, as categories, would, in such a case, be said to be confounded with X, in this case something like "size of consequences."

With this hypothetical other variable X in mind, compare the replicated and unreplicated versions of the same experiment. In the replicated version of the experiment, there will be a large number of individual examples for each category of interest, whereas for the unreplicated design, there will be one example for each category of interest. For the unreplicated design, we can construct substantive rival hypotheses at will, by noting differences between the individual messages other than the difference defined by our classification variable. And any such rival hypothesis is as well supported as the categorical claim involving our intended classification. That is, if C assigns levels C_1 through C_k to k messages, and X assigns levels X_1 through X_k to the same k messages, any pattern of difference among the k messages will support a claim about X as well as it supports a claim about C.

Within the replicated design, the plausibility of the rival hypothesis depends not on whether individual messages differ one from another (as they surely will), but on whether there is some detectable pattern in the way messages as groups differ from one another. To challenge the categorical claim, the X variable must be shown to give at least as good an account of the data as does our intended classification C. Incidental differences among an initial set of k messages would have to recur through additional sets of k messages, and in the same "order," for X to be confounded with C. So, for example, if the first threat and promise differ in "size of consequences," the remaining additional threats and promises must also differ in "size of consequences," and in a consistent way: the large consequences consistently (or at least predominantly) occurring in threats and the small consequences in promises.

Unless the procedure for collecting or generating the individual messages contains some systematic source of bias, we normally assume that any differences recurring throughout the samples within each category are not incidental, but connected in some important way with what the category *is*. Any X put forward as a rival hypothesis must take the form, once messages are replicated, of an alternative classification of the messages or an alternative description of the message classes. The set of Xs that can plausibly be put forward as alternative classifications or alternative descriptions is diminished as (1) the size of the message set grows, (2) the within-category diversity increases, and (3) the particular messages chosen within categories are selected to avoid identifiable confounds.

What nonstructural means could be used to avoid systematic confounds between C and any other variable X? The problem here is precisely analogous to the problem of making comparisons among categories representing individual differences among people. When we want, for example, to evaluate gender differences in communication, it is always possible that the particular men and women observed differ in some other individual characteristic (e.g., educational level) that might account for between-group differences. One might suppose that this problem simply calls for a retreat from causal to correlational claims, but that is not quite right. Unless the men and women observed are representative of their respective populations, even the correlational claim may be unjustified, and besides, retreating from the causal claim means giving up on our research objective. An alternative, commonly used in research on individual differences, is to develop lines of argument that negate some finite class of rival hypotheses, building in the process an increasingly definite presumption in favor of the proposed account of categorical differences.

Perhaps it would be helpful to suspend for a moment some preconceived notions about design and analysis and approach the problem of a categorical comparison armed with nothing but common sense. Let us say that we observe a number of occurrences of each of two types and note that, on the average, outcomes related to occurrences of the first type differ in some respect from occurrences of the second type. Suppose, for example, we notice that people tend to laugh more at story-line jokes than at question–answer jokes. A reasonable person will certainly try to evaluate the possibility that the difference responsible for the different outcomes is not the initial distinction between the occurrences, but some other distinction. For example, such a person might try out certain alternative classifications of jokes, such as incongruity-based humor versus derogation-based humor, to see whether they better fit the differentiations being made by the audience. But having compared other sorts of distinctions to the initial account and found none superior, the person may reasonably act on the belief that outcomes are related to the type of occurrence as initially conjectured. For a reasonable person, this belief should continue to function as a presumption rather than a definite conclusion, and this is just to say that the belief must be continually evaluated against newly recognized rivals. But as long as none of these rivals overcome the presumption, it is reasonable to act on it and unreasonable to ignore it. If the person must choose some type of joke, and would like it to be as well received as possible, the person would be well advised to use the most successful of the available classifications as a basis for choice.

A categorical claim put forward on the basis of a comparison between two large, heterogeneous samples of messages chosen without any identifiable slant should enjoy this sort of presumption. The presumption may be weakly or strongly held, depending on the usual sort of issues: number of observations, number and kind of competing hypotheses considered and rejected, availability of other competing hypotheses, amount of variability within categories relative to variability between categories, procedures used in selecting cases for study. We will later take up some concrete strategies for addressing the last of these issues; as may perhaps be apparent, these strategies must be tailored to the sorts of competing hypotheses we will have to evaluate.

To summarize the discussion so far, I have argued that adding replications to the standard categorical comparison design eliminates case–category confounding as a threat and mitigates threats based on confounding of the category of interest with other variables. A comparison based on many cases from each category is better than a comparison based on a single case from each category. At the same time, we never achieve certainty on the question of whether our present categorization of cases is the best account of what we observe; our generalizations about message classifications have the status of presumptions held strongly or weakly depending on the evidence at hand.

Now, what of the second threat to validity described in Chapter 2, the concealed insufficiency of data? The single-message design, because it has no explicit message replications factor, gives a misleading appearance of corroboration to its categorical claims, by treating the responses of each individual person as independent evidence for the claim. But the individual responses are independent only with respect to a limited domain, namely that defined by the individual message cases observed. A multiple-message design structured along the lines of any of the prototypes described here addresses this threat in two ways.

First, the multiple-message design offers a better basis for generalization by incorporating more cases from the categories of interest. Sufficiency of data within a multiple-message design is dependent upon local circumstances such as the amount of within-category variability, but the *least* that can be claimed for a multiple-message design is that it is less insufficient than a single-message design. And each increase in the number of messages observed is an increase in sufficiency, though at some point the increases will become negligible.

Second, the multiple-message design makes explicit the basis for the categorical generalization, by preserving message replications as levels of an explicit factor and using variability among them as an estimate of error. Insufficiency, if present, is not concealed. This is important, because in addition to being able to draw reliable conclusions, we need to be able to assess reliability—to decide, for example, how confident to be of the conclusion. When we incorporate few replications into the design, this fact is taken into account in the usual statistical ways, and its consequences for the confidence we may place in the conclusion are manifest. Increases in the number of replications incorporated pay off in increased statistical power and decreased error of estimate. This is as it should be.

AN EXAMPLE RECONSIDERED

To illustrate the strengths of the replicated categorical comparison, let us return to the experiment on reciprocation of self-disclosure analyzed in Chapter 1. Recall that the claim to be defended was that the acceptability of various forms of reciprocation depends on the intimacy level of the initial disclosure, with low-intimacy disclosures preferring a matching of intimacy level and high-intimacy disclosures preferring a mismatching intimacy level. The weakness in the evidence for this complex claim was that categorical conclusions were drawn from comparisons among individual narratives differing in dimensions other than intimacy level and topical continuity. How would the case be improved if similar results were observed in a replicated design rather than an unreplicated design?

Suppose we were to arrange for 10 replications, that is, 10 identically structured sets of messages. This would not necessarily involve a ten-fold increase in the number of respondents; instead, the available respondents would simply be divided among the replications. It should also be noted that there would not be any particular reason to repeat the original arrangement precisely, and in particular, no need to use the same response messages for both a high-intimacy and a low-intimacy initiation. The incorporation of replications makes several slightly different designs feasible. An experiment with 10 replications could be structured in several different ways which would each offer some distinct advantage over the unreplicated design.

One way of arranging the materials would be to write 10 high-intimacy and 10 low-intimacy initiations, and then, for each of these 20 initiations, to generate a response of each of the four crucial types. This would mean a total of 100 messages, but it should be noted on the one hand that they would not be particularly difficult to produce, and on the other hand that they could be generated in a variety of ways that would minimize the demands on the researcher's creativity. Each of the 20 initiations would have its own set of responses matched and mismatched on topic and intimacy level. These message sets (each consisting of an initiation and four responses) would be considered levels of the replication factor, and they would be nested within the levels of initiation intimacy level but crossed with response type. (Since each of four responses within a set would be paired with a common initiation, this is just right.) Methods for analysis of a design of this type will be reserved for Chapter 4.

Another way of arranging the materials would be to write a much larger number of initiations, but pair each initiation with only one of the four response types. To produce 10 dialogues in each cell, this would require 80 dialogues, 40 initiated by high-intimacy disclosures and 40 by low-intimacy disclosures. Dialogues would be considered levels of the replication factor and would be nested under combinations of levels of the three factors. An advantage of this arrangement is that since the initiations would not be repeated over dialogues, there would be nothing to prevent having respondents rate several different dialogues.

Still another possibility is to *begin* by writing 80 response messages (40 each of low-intimacy and high-intimacy disclosures), and to randomly assign these response messages to treatment conditions. The initiations (matching or mismatching on topic and intimacy level) could be written to produce the assigned context for the response, so that instead of writing a response to, say, match the topic of the initiation but mismatch its intimacy level, the initiation would be written to match the topic of the response and mismatch its intimacy level. This may seem a matter of no importance, but in fact it has some specifiable advantages over the original procedure. Assigning response messages at random answers all objections that flow from a suspicion of systematic biases in the quality of response messages written with prior knowledge of the treatment group, a topic to be treated more fully in Chapter 7.

How would these alternative designs help matters? Let us suppose that the results were the same as in the original study. Which rival hypotheses would be disarmed and which would not? Recall that the major critique was that the response messages gave particularistic information about the speaker that might plausibly account for differences in attractiveness, quite independently of any systematic consequence of topic or intimacy-matching. In all three versions of the replicated design proposed here as an improvement, there are resources for making an independent assessment of "content" effects and "categorical" effects. Specifically, content effects should show up not only as differences from one *group* of messages to another, but also as differences *within* groups of messages. By calculating the differences among responses within groups, we have a basis for estimating how much difference to expect between group means. Should the differences between the groups exceed what might be expected on the basis of differences within groups, we could certainly disarm the objection that apparent treatment differences reflected only differences in content from response to response.

Our discussion of the self-disclosure experiment gave a rather concrete cast to the idea of "content" effects. Specifically, we noted that while one of the four response messages contained information about the speaker that was basically positive, the other three response messages contained information that might be considered rather negative (mentions of morally questionable or even criminal behavior). Would the alternative design proposed here offer protection against such a critique? The mere inclusion of multiple messages per cell does not guarantee any such protection, of course, since we could very well write only positive narratives for one cell and only discrediting narratives for the other three cells. But notice how random assignment of response messages to cells contributes to disarming this threat. If the entire pool of response messages is prepared without regard for experimental treatment, there can be no strong basis for believing that randomly formed subsets of the messages are systematically biased in any way. Now, that is not true for the initiation messages, but as it is the response messages, not the initiation messages, that are rated for acceptability, the potential damage to the claims about response types is virtually nullified.

There is one sort of confounding that is not handled by any of the improved designs: the confounding of intimacy level with reciprocity of intimacy level. If we were to find, as the original experiment did, that the acceptability of reciprocating intimacy depends on the intimacy level of the initiating turn, we would be very hard put to distinguish between two possible conclusions: first, that matching is desirable with low-intimacy initiations but undesirable with high-intimacy initiations, and second, that low-intimacy responses are preferred regardless of the intimacy-level of the initiation. But the difficulty of disentangling these two conclusions comes not from confounding, but from the fact that they represent two ways of describing what amounts in practical terms to the same thing: a preference across contexts for low-intimacy responses to self-disclosures. If it were important for theoretical reasons to force a differentiation between the two conclusions, we could, of course, conduct a context-free comparison of the high- and low-intimacy disclosures, precisely parallel to the manipulation checks in the original study, hoping to show that their "absolute" differences in acceptability were not sufficient to account for their differences in acceptability in the context of low- and high-intimacy initiations.

SUMMARY

This chapter proposes a simple solution to the problems of validity that plague unreplicated categorical comparisons. The solution is to conduct experiments using multiple messages within each category of interest. In such a design, estimates of categorical effects remain confounded with case effects, but since the presence of a replication factor allows for independent estimation of the case effects, the confounding can be addressed statistically, and very convincing arguments can be constructed against the suspicion that category means differ simply as a consequence of uncontrolled case-to-case difference.

The possible confounding of a classification variable with some other classification variable is another matter, one not amenable to structural solution. But this problem too is mitigated by incorporation of multiple messages within each category of interest. A general presumption in favor of a proposed categorical interpretation can be built through analytic/argumentative strategies available uniquely within a replicated design; specifically, a replicated design can be reanalyzed under various reclassifications of the replications, so as to demonstrate that no plausible alternative account can be found for the differences observed between one category and another.

Replicated designs, properly analyzed, also solve the problem of concealed insufficiency of data, not only by increasing the sufficiency of the data in the first place, but also by making hypothesis tests responsive to the number of messages examined.

FOUR

Replicated Treatment Comparisons

More or less distinct from the class of research problems addressed in Chapter 3 are a class of problems related to evaluation of the effects of a "treatment" on messages of some sort. The research situation to which this chapter responds comes about when we envision individual messages as being open to certain strategic variations whose effects we would like to be able to anticipate. This sort of research situation might arise, for example, in connection with questions about the relative effectiveness of different presentation media given a fixed text, questions about the relative effectiveness of forms of expression given a basic core of content, and questions about the relative effectiveness of alternative types of appeals given a fixed objective. Whereas the previous chapter dealt with explorations of variables that define distinct classes of messages, this chapter deals with variables that are conceptualized as decisions to be made within the context of any given message within a class.

Recall from Chapter 2 that the standard approach to such research problems is to manipulate the variable of interest within the context of a single illustrative message, called the "kernel" message. The standard design is characterized by administration of the treatment variable to a single kernel message from the domain of interest. Such a design offers manifestly inadequate resources for arguing general claims about the effect of the treatment. In Chapter 2, I introduced three pervasive threats to the validity of generic interpretations of the outcomes of experiments conducted within the framework of the standard design: superfluous variation, "gestalt" effects, and unexamined variability in the treatment effect. In this chapter, my purpose is to propose a general design solution and to explain how it responds to each of these threats.

DESIGN PROTOTYPES

The common feature of all designs to be discussed in this chapter is that they involve a crossing of the treatment variable with a message replications factor. We will call these designs *replicated treatment comparisons*. Each will have a treatment variable, T, with at least two levels. Levels of the treatment variable will be denoted when necessary by T with a subscript number.

Each design will also have a *message replications factor*, denoted M, with levels, M_1, M_2, . . . , M_m. The levels of the replications factor are not individual concrete messages, as in the designs of Chapter 3, but message sets created by applying the various treatments to a kernel message. The messages within a set are alternative versions of the kernel message. Another name for the replicated treatments comparison would be the *matched-messages design* (Jackson & Jacobs, 1983), for in any of these designs we can see the messages representing one treatment level as being "matched" with the messages representing other treatment levels.

For example, if the treatment variable is language intensity, each message set would represent several related versions of the same general message content, namely, the same speech or essay with only variations in isolated words and phrases. If the treatment variable is presentation medium, each message set would represent a single "text" presented in several different ways, for example, in print, in audiotape performance, in videotape performance, and in live performance. To say that messages are crossed with treatments is simply to say that each distinct message replication appears at each level of the treatment variable. Such an arrangement is analogous to a standard repeated-measures design in which respondents are said to be crossed with treatments.

The most widely applicable design for evaluating message treatments will be a straightforward generalization from the standard controlled-message design—an assembly of m repetitions of the standard design into a $t \times m$ independent-groups design. In the replicated version of the standard design, message replications are crossed with treatments and respondents are nested within cells defined by the crossing of treatments and messages.

How is a crossing of messages with treatments achieved? The structure of a replicated treatment design can be better understood by thinking abstractly about the production of the experimental messages. The process of manipulating a message variable within a single kernel message involves three steps: the development of the kernel itself, the specification of a "treatment space" within the kernel, and the creation of "treatment segments" to insert into the treatment space. Applying this set of three steps to a number of different kernels produces the replicated treatment comparisons. In other words, a crossing of messages with treatments is accomplished by gathering a number of kernel messages and modifying each of these to produce the required number of versions. For example, to compare one-sided and two-sided argumentation, an initial pool of one-sided arguments might be gathered, then modified to produce partnered two-sided arguments. Alternatively, kernel messages might be gathered without respect to their initial value on the sidedness variable and modified as needed to fill out the cells of the design. Either way, the end result should be a one-sided and a two-sided version of each kernel message.

The nesting of respondents within cells means simply that each person is presented with one and only one concrete message, and the reasons for choosing such an arrangement have more to do with the practical limitations imposed by the message materials than with any principled arguments. This would be the sort of arrangement that we would likely choose if the messages presented to respondents were fairly long or complex, or if the dependent measure involved difficult or time-consuming judgments. As we will see shortly, nesting respondents within cells presents fewer statistical difficulties than other arrangements, but it does not, of course, follow that this is a "preferred" arrangement in any general sense.

Figure 4.1 schematizes the design, and the sense in which it can be said to be a generalization of the standard unreplicated design should be clear: The replicated version with m messages is the structural equivalent of m independently conducted unreplicated treatment comparisons, assembled into an m-layered stack.

Such a design obviously offers resources for examining not only the average effect of the treatment, but also the variability of the treatment from one message to another. There are four separable sources of variance in the design: treatments, messages, the treatment × message interaction, and respondents within groups. The treatment × message interaction represents the variability of the treatment effect

	Treatment 1	Treatment 2
Message 1	[Version 1] Audience 1	[Version 2] Audience m + 1
Message 2	[Version 1] Audience 2	[Version 2] Audience m + 2
⋮	⋮	⋮
Message m	[Version 1] Audience m	[Version 2] Audience $2m$

FIGURE 4.1. Messages-by-treatments design with independent groups. Note. Each audience is a separate sample of persons; m = the number of kernel messages.

from message to message, and besides being interesting in its own right, this effect has implications for estimation and testing of the treatment main effect.

The problem is to estimate the treatment difference, and with respect to this task both messages and respondents should normally be considered random.[1] This design is easily recognized as a textbook case of a "mixed-model" factorial design (one factor fixed, one factor random). An appropriate test of the treatment effect can be formed as allows (see appendix, Design 5):

$$F = MS_T / MS_{T \times M}, \ df = t - 1, \ (m - 1)(t - 1)$$

Alternative designs differ from one another primarily in the allocation of respondents to messages and/or treatments. If, for example, the message sets are such that all versions within a set can or should or must be presented to a single audience, we may nest respondents within messages and cross them with treatment levels. Suppose, for example, that we wish to evaluate some consequence of two ways of responding to a conversational opening, and the explicit comparison between the two ways of responding is important in fixing the meaning of the opening. Then we might ask each respondent to look at both of a pair of responses and to evaluate each separately. This arrangement, schematized in Figure 4.2, is only slightly more complicated than the first arrangement, and when circumstances allow it, it has the advantage of making better use of the available respondents. The test of the treatment effect, as before, involves a ratio of treatment variance to treatment × message interaction variance.

If it is impossible to present respondents with multiple messages within a set, it may still be reasonable to present respondents with multiple messages, perhaps all of the messages within a single level

	Treatment 1	Treatment 2
Message 1	[Version 1] Audience 1	[Version 2] Audience 1
Message 2	[Version 1] Audience 2	[Version 2] Audience 2
⋮	⋮	⋮
Message *m*	[Version 1] Audience *m*	[Version 2] Audience *m*

FIGURE 4.2. Messages-by-treatments design with multiple response: Treatments factor repeated. Note. Each audience responds to all of the messages within a set.

of the treatment. This would be appropriate if the messages were rather short and the response task not very demanding. Suppose, for example, our research question concerned the dependency of a speaker's perceived interpersonal competence on some feature of complaint responses (say, a simple paraphrase of the complaint), and our treatment involved the insertion of the feature into a basic response. A message pair would consist of two two-turn dialogues (the complaint and the response), with the members of the pair varied through the presence or absence (in the response) of a brief paraphrase of the complaint. We obviously would not want to present a respondent with two nearly identical dialogues to evaluate, and indeed, we might prefer not to allow respondents in the control condition to see any messages at all from the experimental condition. This sort of situation could give rise to the design schematized in Figure 4.3, with the respondents factor P crossed with messages but nested under treatments.

As might be anticipated from the discussions in Chapter 3, this non-hierarchical arrangement of the two replication factors commits

	Treatment 1	Treatment 2
Message 1	[Version 1] Audience 1	[Version 2] Audience 2
Message 2	[Version 1] Audience 1	[Version 2] Audience 2
⋮	⋮	⋮
Message *m*	[Version 1] Audience 1	[Version 2] Audience 2

FIGURE 4.3. Messages-by-treatments design with multiple response: Messages factor repeated. Note: Audience 1 responds to all version 1 messages and audience 2 to all version 2 messages.

the researcher to constructing a quasi F ratio in order to test the treatment differences (see Appendix, Design 6).

$$F' = (MS_T + MS_{M \times P/T})/(MS_{T \times M} + MS_{P/T})$$

Degrees of freedom for any such ratio must be approximated. Winer (1971) takes the nearest integer value of a complex function of the component mean squares and their degrees of freedom, as follows. If the mean squares added together to produce either the numerator or denominator of the F' ratio are denoted u and v, then the corresponding degrees of freedom are obtained by taking the nearest integer value of the quantity

$$df = [(u + v)^2]/[(u^2/df_u) + (v^2/df_v)]$$

An arrangement that offers some practical economies in exchange for some considerable statistical difficulties is to administer all of the various treatment conditions to each subject, each time using a different replication. For example, if there are four treatments to be compared and some large number of replications to which all four treatments are applied, each respondent could get a complete set of four messages, representing a subset of the available replications and all of the treatments, as shown in Figure 4.4. Examples of this sort of design appear in recent studies by Shimanoff (1987) and Thomas and Parpal (1987). The complexities involved in such an arrangement would require some care on the part of the experimenter to avoid confounding the effects involving replications with other effects in the design; the general approach is to treat them as a Latin-square or similar arrangement.

Of course these are not the only possible arrangements, but for now the more useful continuation may be to consider the ways in which other message factors might combine with these plans to create multifactor designs.

	Treatment 1	Treatment 2	Treatment 3	Treatment 4
Message 1	Person 1	Person 2	Person 3	Person 4
Message 2	Person 2	Person 3	Person 4	Person 1
Message 3	Person 3	Person 4	Person 1	Person 2
Message 4	Person 4	Person 1	Person 2	Person 3

FIGURE 4.4. Latin-square arrangement. Note: This arrangement is repeated as needed with additional messages and respondents.

The basic principle underlying all modifications of the designs presented here and in Chapter 3 is that any "cell" composed of levels of message variables should contain multiple examples. An experiment involving a single classification variable or a single treatment variable requires multiple cases within each class or multiple replications of the treatment in order to justify generic interpretations of the comparisons involved. An experiment involving two message variables must contain replications sufficient to justify generic conclusions about each main effect, and also about the interaction, and it will therefore not be appropriate to have a single concrete message appear at each combination of levels.

We will consider two designs each involving two message variables. Generalization of the underlying design principles will be clear enough from these examples to make additional examples unnecessary. For simplicity, subsequent discussion of designs will assume independent groups of respondents (that is, respondents nested within cells), but other arrangements may easily be generalized from the earlier examples.

Consider the class of problems that take the form of an evaluation of a treatment relative to some classification of the messages to which the treatment is to be applied. Two message variables are implied, one classification variable and one treatment variable. This sort of problem might arise as part of an analysis of the generality of a treatment effect or as part of a search for limiting conditions on a strategic principle. For example, an interest in whether the advantage of two-sided argument over one-sided depends on the controversiality of the position taken would involve sidedness as a form of treatment applied to messages and controversiality as a classification factor.

Problems of this sort require examination of the treatment effect at each level of the classification variable, and hence the two message variables are crossed with one another. Since controversiality is not easily manipulated within what might be considered a fixed message, each message case included in the design must appear at one level of controversiality, leading to a nesting of messages under categories. But message cases may still be crossed with the treatment variable (and they *should* be whenever possible). This sort of design, simplified through omission of the respondents factor, is schematized in Figure 4.5.

Notice that a single message within each level of the classification variable would make all of the categorical comparisons vulnerable to case–category confounding and would also confound the case-to-case variations in treatment effects with the classification × treatment interaction. For this reason, a classification-by-treatment design with a

		Treatment 1	Treatment 2
Category 1	Message 1	[Version 1]	[Version 2]
	Message 2	[Version 1]	[Version 2]
	⋮		
	Message m	[Version 1]	[Version 2]
Category 2	Message $m + 1$	[Version 1]	[Version 2]
	Message $m + 2$	[Version 1]	[Version 2]
	⋮		
	Message $2m$	[Version 1]	[Version 2]

FIGURE 4.5. Treatment-by-classification design with replications. Note: The respondents factor has been omitted for simplicity of presentation.

single message at each classification level does not substitute for a replicated treatment comparison design.

A final class of research problems to consider are those in which we are interested in the simultaneous application of two or more treatments to individual messages. This sort of problem might come about through an interest in the cooperation of two strategic choices, or through an interest in the way one choice might limit or depend on another. For example, suppose we were interested in the cooperation of fear arousal and proposal specificity (as in Rogers & Mewborn, 1976), on the hypothesis that it is no use arousing a great deal of fear unless some specific remedy is available. The research question points to two strategic variations, either of which could be applied separately to any given message, but both of which could be applied simultaneously within messages. A question of this type often springs from a suspicion that the effect of one of the strategic variations may depend on the other strategic variation.

For research problems of this sort, involving simultaneous manipulation of two treatment variables, the usual arrangement will be a crossing of the treatment variables with one another and with the messages replication factor. What this means is that the entire batch of kernel messages will be subjected to both manipulations in such a way as to produce a number of versions equal to the product of the numbers of levels of the two treatment variables. We have been using T to refer to a single treatment variable; let us refer to the other as T'. If T has t levels and T' has t' levels, then each message set will include $t \times t'$ versions of the kernel message. The treatment comparison for T involves averaging not only across many respondents and many messages, but also across t' versions of each message. A complementary situation holds for evaluation of the effect of T'. But since T and T' will ordinarily both be considered "fixed" factors, this complexity does not pose any serious difficulties for analysis of the experiment. The inclusion of messages as a replication factor introduces some difficulty, but no more than for the single-treatment design considered above.

The design schematized in Figure 4.6, if implemented as an independent-groups design, has four factors and eight separable sources of variance: T, T', the messages replication factor M, the $T \times T'$, $T \times M$, $T' \times M$, and $T \times T' \times M$ interactions, and the respondents nested within cells. Tests of each effect of interest must take account of the messages replication factor, leading to a different choice of error terms for each of the F tests that might be of interest (see Appendix, Design 7). For the main effects:

$$F = MS_T/MS_{T \times M}, \, df = t - 1, \, (t - 1)(m - 1)$$

and

$$F = MS_{T'}/MS_{T' \times M}, \, df = t' - 1, \, (t' - 1)(m - 1)$$

	Perspective 1			
	Treatment 1		Treatment 2	
	Treatment A	Treatment B	Treatment A	Treatment B
Message 1	[Version 1a]	[Version 1b]	[Version 2a]	[Version 2b]
Message 2	[Version 1a]	[Version 1b]	[Version 2a]	[Version 2b]
⋮				
Message *m*	[Version 1a]	[Version 1b]	[Version 2a]	[Version 2b]

	Perspective 2		
		Factor 1	
		Treatment 1	Treatment 2
Factor 2	Treatment A	[Version 1a, all messages]	[Version 2a, all messages]
	Treatment B	[Version 1b, all messages]	[Version 2b, all messages]

FIGURE 4.6. Treatment-by-treatment design with replications from two alternative perspectives.

where t is the number of levels of treatment variable T, t' is the number of levels of treatment variable T', and m is the number of kernel messages.

For the $T \times T'$ interaction:

$$F = MS_{T \times T'}/MS_{T \times T' \times M},$$
$$df = (t - 1)(t' - 1), (t - 1)(t' - 1)(m - 1)$$

HOW THE REPLICATED DESIGN ADDRESSES THREATS TO VALID INFERENCE

Evaluation of the effect of a message-treatment variable presents the researcher with two difficult problems: One is isolation of the treatment variable from other possible sources of dependent variation (appearing in Chapter 2 in discussions of superfluous variation and gestalt effects), and the other is coping with case-to-case variability in the treatment effect itself (appearing in Chapter 2 as unexamined variability). The basic solution advanced in the preceding section is the same as in Chapter 3: Incorporate multiple messages into the design as replications of the basic comparison. How does this solution address the threats to validity outlined in Chapter 2? We need an abstract description of the problem in order to see the way in which the solution constitutes a response.

Imagine a pool of messages to which the treatment might be applied; normally, this pool is not a finite collection of individual messages, but an abstract category with an infinite number of exemplars, such as "persuasive messages," "self-disclosures," "threats," and the like. For any message drawn from the pool, let us suppose that there is a limit on how much difference the treatment can make for that particular message. We can think of this as the message's receptiveness or susceptibility to the treatment, as previously shown in Figure 2.5. This general limit could be the same for all messages, but there is neither any reason, nor any need, to suppose that that is so. Further, any particular implementation of the treatment, even within the context of a fixed message, can be better or worse at isolating the treatment variable from other influences, so we should begin with the presumption that any individual manipulation may represent more than one causal variable, whether through superfluous variation, or through gestalt effects, or through both.

If we entertain the possibility that different messages are differently susceptible to the treatment, it is clear that generic statements about the treatment are intended as statements about the "expected" effect of the treatment—the average effect—and that no single message, however carefully controlled, offers any sort of basis for a conclusion at this level. In Figure 2.5 the treatment effect for individual messages is pictured as normally distributed with an average effect representing a general preference for one treatment or another, but with the effect of the treatment on any individual message somewhere above or below the average. An individual message selected for study might be unusually receptive to the treatment, giving us an estimate of the treatment effect well above the average, or unusually insensitive to the treatment, giving us a value well below the average. And the results obtained with the individual message offer no resources at all for guessing where the message itself falls within the distribution of effect sizes.

Multiple comparisons allow a search for central tendency, and more importantly, they allow us to take into account explicitly the manifest instability of the effect. The response to unexamined variability in the treatment effect is to *examine* it.

The variations introduced incidentally to the intended variation may be seen as a sort of imperfection in the operationalization of the treatment variable, something not unlike measurement error. If these incidental variations are random, their effect will be to make the variance in actual implementations greater than the true variance in receptivity to the treatment, but they will not change the average value of the treatment. So long as there is no *systematic* confounding of other variables with the intendedly manipulated variable, sheer multiplicity solves this problem in the same way that it solves the first, because the contribution of the extra variations is made visible in the variability of the treatment effect from replication to replication. It appears, in other words, confounded (more or less innocuously) with the underlying variation in the true effect size for individual messages. Statistically, both sources of variation appear as treatment × message interaction in a replicated treatments comparison.

In an unreplicated design, there is no way at all to notice, measure, or correct for either of these sorts of variation. In a design with multiple replications, the variability of the treatment effect from message to message is straightforwardly measurable, the usual means being calculation of a treatment × message interaction effect but alternative means being available through such procedures as calculations of the variance in standardized effect sizes (Hedges & Olkin, 1985; see related discussion of this point in Jackson, O'Keefe, Jacobs, & Brashers, 1989, and in Jackson, 1991).

Now including multiple replications within a design does not eliminate the message-to-message variability in treatment effect, if any. Indeed, in *any* sample of messages, the average treatment effect will be influenced by which particular messages were included in the sample—a direct analogy to sampling error introduced by the particular human respondents observed. As might be anticipated, a multiple-message design reduces "message sampling error" as compared to a design with a message sample size of 1. The more messages included in the experiment, the more reliable the resulting estimate of the average treatment effect (Jackson et al., 1989). But equally importantly, the inclusion of multiple messages allows us to qualify our interpretations of the average treatment effect in terms of the measurable error involved in estimating it. Multiple messages provide a basis—entirely absent in an unreplicated design—for estimating how that average will vary from sample to sample. The variability in treatment effects within the sample is the basis for the estimate of how the average will vary from sample to sample—a familiar pattern in statistical inference.

Likewise, the inclusion of multiple replications within a design does not eliminate superfluous variations or gestalt effects from the individual implementations of the treatment; however, it does limit the plausibility of *rival hypotheses* based on superfluous variation and gestalt effects. As with the replicated categorical comparison designs, the replicated treatment comparison designs offer a partial structural remedy, and open up opportunities for additional, nonstructural attacks on the problem. Superfluous variations and gestalt effects that are unsystematic and idiosyncratically associated with the treatment are disarmed by the replicated design, because their influence is taken into account in the now-measurable variability in treatment effect from replication to replication. Notice that in each design considered in this chapter, variability in the treatment effect from replication to replication figures into testing of the treatment effect, as the error term for the F test.

But what about features of the treatment that systematically confound the variable of interest with some other causal variable? Superfluous variations that have been systematically associated with the treatment for some reason cannot be eliminated through repetition of the same procedure with other materials, as Morley (1988) has correctly pointed out.

Within the framework of a single message subjected to a treatment, we can imagine four sorts of influences: the general effect of the variable of interest, the case-specific limitation on that effect, the joint effect of all haphazard superfluous variations for that particular implementation of the treatment, and the joint effect of all systematic superfluous variations (affecting this message just as it would every other). The first influence is what we want to estimate, and the other three are various sorts of obstacles to getting a reasonable estimate. Sheer multiplicity handles the first two obstacles, but not the third. The third obstacle must be addressed through nonstructural means, and this is true not only for replicated and unreplicated message designs, but for every imaginable social scientific experiment.

As with simple categorical comparisons, the opportunities for confounding an intended variation with an unintended variation are inherent in our currently available frameworks for conceptualizing and differentiating messages. No structural solution to the problem presented by this sort of confounding is possible, nor is it likely that such a solution will ever be possible (D. O'Keefe, 1987). However, as with categorical comparison designs, the basic framework of a replicated treatments comparison draws attention to the problem of confounding and invites a variety of remedies.

To begin with, the reconstruction of the message as a sample instantiation of a treatment (rather than as a nonproblematic embodiment of a concept) invites attention to sampling issues. The first step toward isolation of the treatment variable of interest is to avoid choosing messages in such a way as to encourage too much uniformity in the implementation of the treatment. Not only should we try to begin with relatively diverse samples of base messages, but we should also generally try to avoid too mechanical an approach to the creation of contrasting message versions. As Morley (1988) has pointed out, opportunities for systematic confounding are maximized by experimenting on a set of messages all written and subjected to treatment by the experimenter. If the treatment procedure (say, insertion of two-sided material into initially one-sided arguments) repeats an unexamined superfluous variation in message after message, the one-sided and two-sided arguments may differ, not because of sidedness, but because of the other variable slipped into each message. Note that at the level of single messages, it is virtually impossible to preclude all confounds of this sort, but at the level of multiple messages, reasonable care in the development of message sets limits vulnerability to this sort of confounding. Some concrete suggestions for the development of experimental message sets are offered in Chapter 7.

When multiple replications of the treatment comparison are available, it is also possible to consider the question of confounding in a post hoc way. Whether because some particular confound is suspected or because the message-to-message variations in treatment effect are themselves suspicious looking, multiplicity offers the possibility of partitioning a set of messages in various ways to evaluate the plausibility of rival accounts of the effect. For example, suppose we have observed that two-sided essays are more persuasive than their one-sided counterparts, and suspect that it is not sidedness per se, but length, that accounts for the difference. If we have a large and diverse set of replications of the sidedness treatment, it may be possible to partition them into those that add length with the inclusion of two-sided materials and those that equate length across versions. If the advantage of two-sidedness holds only for two-sided messages that are longer than their one-sided counterparts, the rival account gains plausibility, while an advantage for two-sidedness that holds within both subsets is persuasive evidence against the rival account.[2] Eliminating rival accounts one by one in this fashion can obviously never establish that the manipulation is free from confounding, but it can create an increasingly strong presumption in favor of the "winning" account. As with categorical comparisons, the process of defending a claim about a treatment effect is open-ended, and at any given point in time, we hold generalizations about treatment effects as presumptions justified by experience to date.

Ultimately, the barrier to eliminating systematic confounding in message experiments as in all other research is our ability to notice it. Our protection against confounding is always limited by the sophistication of our descriptions of our subject matter and our understanding of what things could or might make a difference. But within those limits, it makes sense to try to minimize the opportunities for systematic confounding and to maximize our own possibilities for noticing it. Adding multiple replications to message treatment designs changes our situation from one in which any single concrete contrast may carry an indefinitely large number of important or unimportant variations to one in which the manipulation *procedure* can be inspected apart from the individual concrete contrasts. Apart from blatantly uncontrolled procedures, a replicated design offers no reason to believe that there is, in fact, any confounding. These are very different situations, and the difference between them is the contribution of the replicated design.

SUMMARY

Unreplicated treatment comparisons can be repaired straightforwardly by the incorporation of replications of the treatment across multiple messages. Superfluous variations and gestalt effects introduced by the treatment, if random in their effects on the outcome, are on the one hand mitigated by increases in the "message sample" size, and on the other hand taken into account statistically when messages are treated explicitly as a replication factor. Where unreplicated designs suffer from unexamined variability in the effects to be estimated, replicated designs examine the variability and take it into account in measuring and evaluating treatment effects. A variety of designs crossing message replications with treatments are described and discussed.

FIVE

Statistical Analysis of Replicated Experiments

The problem we confront in research on message categories is that of drawing a conclusion about two or more abstract classes of messages that can be disassociated from the particular concrete exemplars taken to represent each class. This would be no problem at all if messages within the categories of interest were equivalent with respect to the outcome variables of interest. Unfortunately, on both intuitive and empirical grounds, we must entertain the possibility that messages within categories are not uniform with respect to the outcome variables of interest (see the extensive discussion of this point in Jackson et al., 1989). Differences among message categories or effects of message treatments must be assumed to be averages of values that vary within the domains of the message variables, and these averages are subject to variation related to the particular samples observed.

The two preceding chapters presume that messages incorporated as replications within experiments will be treated as levels of a random factor in the statistical analysis. The factor may be labeled "messages," "message sets," or "replications." The basic positive rationale for treating the replication factor as a random factor is that replications are a source of error variance in the estimation of the categorical differences or the treatment effects. If messages within categories are not uniform, either in their preexisting characteristics or in their responsiveness to treatments, estimates of categorical differences and treatment effects will vary depending on which particular message cases happen to be used as a basis for the estimate. Treating messages as levels of a random factor results in tests of categorical differences and treatment effects that take into account message sampling error in these estimates.

In this chapter, I will describe three analytic possibilities available within an analysis-of-variance framework once message replications have been incorporated into the experiment. Of these possibilities, one will be advanced as clearly preferable to the other two; specifically, the treatment of messages as a random effect will be advocated as the best of the analytic strategies. The same argument (contextualized differently) was advanced by Clark (1973), and there followed a great deal of discussion. I will review and discuss the major objections that have been raised against this suggestion. In Chapter 6, I will consider alternative statistical procedures for dealing with multiple estimates of a difference or an effect.

ANALYTIC POSSIBILITIES AND THEIR CONSEQUENCES FOR TESTING

Assuming that an experiment includes message replications, the replications factor can be handled in three quite different ways. First, the factor can be ignored entirely, so that any individual observation is identified with a particular treatment condition and a particular human subject, but not with its particular message. Second, the factor can be considered as having "fixed" levels, so that effects involving replications can be estimated like any other effect. Third, the factor can be considered as "random," a consequence of which is that effects involving replications figure as error terms in testing hypotheses about treatment variables.

The first of these alternatives—ignoring the replications factor —is generally inappropriate, because it rolls variance in response due to individual replications into the estimate of some other effect in the design (Jackson, O'Keefe & Jacobs, 1988; see also Kenny & Judd, 1986). The incorporation of multiple replications into an experiment is motivated by the belief that it makes a difference what particular replication is used to embody the treatment variable or its levels. If the replications factor is not retained in the analysis, the variance contributed by replications must be (mis)attributed to some other effect in the design.

The second and third alternatives both retain replications as an explicit factor, but differ in what is assumed about the relationship of replication effects to treatment effects. Treating replications as random assumes that the particular replications used in the experiment are a source of error in estimation of the treatment effect, analogous to respondents. Treating replications as fixed assumes that replications are not a source of error in estimation of the treatment effect. Sums of squares and mean squares computed for each effect in a design are indifferent to whether replications are regarded as fixed or random; however, the decision to treat replications as fixed or as random affects both the estimation of variance components and the testing of hypotheses involving the treatment effects. The differences between these two forms of analysis will be greater or smaller depending on the degree to which the treatment effect does in fact differ from replication to replication and depending on how many replications are examined; in some cases, it may not matter much which is chosen, but we will be considering which form of analysis is the better general policy.

To see exactly what is involved in the choice of analytic strategy, we will consider once again the two principal design prototypes, the categorical comparison (messages nested under classifications) and the treatment comparison (messages crossed with treatments). For simplicity of presentation, we will assume in each case a single independent variable (one classification variable or one treatment variable) and a nesting of human respondents within levels of the replications factor. A preliminary comparison among the three statistical options can be made by examining the computations and choices of test statistics that would follow from each option.

Analysis of Replicated Categorical Comparison Designs

In the replicated categorical comparison, the experiment consists of a classification factor, a replications factor nested under classifications, and a respondents factor nested under replications. What we will call Option A ignores the messages replication factor, treating respondents as being nested under classifications; thus, the analysis of variance results in a breakdown of the total sum of squares into a between-groups component based on between-categories differences (denoted SS_C) and a within-groups component based on deviations of individual responses from category means (denoted $SS_{P/C}$, the slash in P/C indicating that respondents are considered as nested within categories). Options B and C retain the replications factor as a separate variance source, so that the analysis of variance results in a breakdown into the between-groups component (SS_C), a messages-within-categories component ($SS_{M/C}$), and the respondents-within-groups component ($SS_{P/CM}$). Notice that the definition of the within-groups component changes depending on whether the message replication factor is retained or ignored, since "group" can be defined either with respect to one replication within a category or with respect to a category as a whole. As can perhaps be anticipated, the portion of the variance attributed to messages in Options B and C is simply lumped with the respondents variance under Option A. Option A, B, and C analyses are illustrated below for hypothetical data.

To the point represented in Table 5.1, the Option B and Option C analyses are indistinguishable. The sums of squares and mean squares calculated for any effect in the design depend only upon what other effects are in the design, not on whether the effects are considered fixed or random. But notice that Option A, which ignores the messages factor, must nevertheless find a source to hang the messages variance on: The total variance among the 50 scores is a fixed quantity that must somehow be allocated among the sources suggested by the underlying model.

The difference between Options B and C is in how the category differences are evaluated, that is, in how one tests the category differences or estimates their magnitude. As is well known, the nature of the statistical analysis depends on (and implies) an underlying statistical model, that is, a theoretical model of the composition of a score in terms of effects and errors. If μ is the mean of the dependent variable in the relevant population of cases, κ_i is the deviation of the category

TABLE 5.1. Three Analytic Options Illustrated Numerically

Data (n per cell = 5)

Category A	Cell statistics		Category B	Cell statistics	
Message 1	$X = 15$	$SS = 32$	Message 6	$X = 13$	$SS = 30$
Message 2	$X = 10$	$SS = 42$	Message 7	$X = 14$	$SS = 16$
Message 3	$X = 12$	$SS = 16$	Message 8	$X = 11$	$SS = 42$
Message 4	$X = 15$	$SS = 30$	Message 9	$X = 18$	$SS = 26$
Message 5	$X = \ 8$	$SS = 26$	Message 10	$X = 14$	$SS = 32$

Analysis: Sums of squares and mean squares

	Option A		Option B		Option C	
Source	SS	MS	SS	MS	SS	MS
Category	50	50	50	50	50	50
Messages	—	—	320	40	320	40
Subjects	612	12.75	292	7.3	292	7.3
TOTAL	662		662		662	

i mean from μ, γ_{ij} is the deviation of the message j mean from its category mean, and ϵ_{ijk} is the deviation of the kth observation from the mean of message j within category i, then both Options B nd C model the individual score X_{ijk} as follows:

$$X_{ijk} = \mu + \kappa_i + \gamma_{ij} + \epsilon_{ijk}$$

On both Option B and Option C (and also, of course, on Option A, which differs from the others in omitting the term representing the message effect), the ϵs are assumed to be a source of error in estimation of the κs. Option C treats the individual messages included in the experiment as analogous to the individual respondents, that is, as a source of error in estimation of the κs. Option B does not; that is, Option B discounts the categorical differences by an amount representing the human sampling error, but not by an amount representing the message sampling error. This is reflected in the expected mean squares, shown in Table 5.2 below. Expected mean squares are given for each effect in the design as generated by each model: Option A, with messages ignored entirely; Option B, with messages treated as fixed; and Option C, with messages treated as random.[1]

For the researcher's purpose, the difference between Option A and the other two options is in how the within-groups variance is computed: as deviations from category means or as deviations from message-within-category means. The difference between Option B and Option C is in how the between-categories differences are *tested*: For Option B, the F ratio used in testing the category differences is the category mean square divided by the respondents (within-groups) mean square, while for Option C it is the category mean square

TABLE 5.2. Expected Mean Squares for Three Options

Option A (messages ignored)	Category	$mn\sigma_\kappa^2$		$+ \sigma_\epsilon^2$
	Respondents			σ_ϵ^2
Option B (messages fixed)	Category	$mn\sigma_\kappa^2$		$+ \sigma_\epsilon^2$
	Messages		$n\sigma_\pi^2$	$+ \sigma_\epsilon^2$
	Respondents			σ_ϵ^2
Option C (messages random)	Category	$mn\sigma_\kappa^2$	$+ n\sigma_\pi^2$	$+ \sigma_\epsilon^2$
	Messages		$n\sigma_\pi^2$	$+ \sigma_\epsilon^2$
	Respondents			σ_ϵ^2

Note: m is the number of message replications per category, and n is the number of respondents per message.

divided by the messages mean square. The three F ratios are formed as follows:

Option A (replications ignored): $F = MS_C/MS_{P/C}$
Option B (replications fixed): $F = MS_C/MS_{P/MC}$
Option C (replications random): $F = MS_C/MS_{M/C}$

For the data shown in Table 5.1, the three analytic options yield marked differences in the value of F and in the test outcome. Ignoring replications, $F(1,48) = 3.92$, $p = .053$; treating replications as fixed, $F(1,40) = 6.85$, $p = .012$; and treating replications as random, $F(1,8) = 1.25$, $p = .296$. Now, these data are only hypothetical, and they do not, of course, establish that there will always be a noticeable difference between the Option B analysis treating message replications as fixed and the Option C analysis treating message replications as random. Nor do they establish that one form of analysis is better than the others; that will require additional discussion. What the example shows is that the three analytic strategies *can* be quite different in their results, and these differences can be very consequential when we come to drawing conclusions about message categories. We should expect the three options to yield different results any time messages within categories are nonuniform in the responses they get.

One question that might reasonably be raised about the discussion so far is how likely it is that a situation of this sort would arise in real data. As might be anticipated, the differences among the three forms of analysis will not always be pronounced. Sometimes, the three analytic options will all yield the same basic outcome: a significant or nonsignificant F. But other times, the three analytic options will diverge. How *often* this will occur is impossible to predict, given how few studies to date have been structured to permit the comparison, but that it *will* occur is certain; in fact, it already *has* occurred in some of my own research.

Consider an example, from an experiment reported by Jackson and Backus (1982). The experiment, a replication of a well-known study reported by Miller, et al. (1977), had a four-leveled independent variable, labeled "interpersonal situation." There were 16 dependent variables, but for purposes of illustration, we will focus on one: ratings of an interpersonal compliance-gaining strategy generally called "negative expertise." Respondents rated the strategy (along with the other 15, of course) for how likely they would be to use it in the given situation. Since compliance-gaining strategies must be embodied in possible messages (and since these must vary topically from situation to situation), we introduced alternative versions of the "negative expertise" strategy as replications nested within situation. For each of the four situations, there were four different "negative expertise" messages; each respondent got one of these four messages, embedded in a long questionnaire with messages representing each of the other 15 strategies.

All three of the analytic options we have considered can be employed within an unweighted means analysis of variance, with the following results for the test of the situation effect:

Replications ignored: $F(3,157) = 8.059$, $p < .001$
Replications fixed: $F(3,145) = 11.164$, $p < .001$
Replications random: $F(3,12) = 2.508$, $p = .108$

This pattern occurred, by the way, not only for the "negative expertise" variable, but with minor deviations for 9 of the 16 dependent variables. What this example shows is that the conclusion drawn about an effect can be profoundly affected by which of the analytic options a researcher chooses in handling a nested replication factor. It does not, of course, show that the conclusion drawn in every case will differ from one option to another. Only a great deal of accumulated research evidence will allow us to tell how often such patterns will occur. Quite likely we will find that *some* message categories have members that are very uniform, while others have members that are very diverse. Sometimes, it really won't make much difference whether the message replications are treated as fixed or random in testing the category effects, because the messages-within-categories error term will be indistinguishable (except for degrees of freedom) from the respondents-within-categories term. If we could be sure that this would be the case, we could of course use any one of the uniform members of the category instead of using multiple replications within categories.

Having noticed that it makes a difference whether messages are or are not taken into account (Option A versus the other two) and that it can also make a difference whether messages are treated as fixed or random (Option B versus Option C), we are left with the question of how to choose an analytic strategy. Which of the three options is best for the purpose of testing the differences among message categories?

It should be clear by now that the answer we give to this question depends upon what we can assume about the effect of the messages studied on our estimate of the category differences. If we acknowledge that our estimate of category differences depends upon which of an indefinitely large set of possible messages we choose to "observe," neither Option A nor Option B can be given any sort of defense. The error terms used in testing the categorical differences under these two options do not contain all of the sources of error that afflict the estimate of the categorical difference. The Option A F ratio demands the Option A assumptions and the Option B F ratio demands the Option B assumptions: specifically, in the former case, that messages make no difference to response and, in the latter case, that the estimates of the categorical differences do not depend on the messages observed. Both Option A and Option B are logically inconsistent with the assumption that the specific messages observed contribute variability to the estimate of categorical differences, the category mean square.

Can we salvage one or the other option by giving up the assumption that messages contribute "error" to our estimates of categorical differences? No. Or at least, not arbitrarily. An assumption of this sort would obviously be untenable just in case the messages can be seen to be nonuniform within their categories, as in the hypothetical data we are considering. The statistical model "assumed" by a method of analysis is accountable to the data; within any data set, we can evaluate empirically the notion that categorical differences are unaffected by message-by-message differences.

Consider once again the data displayed in Table 5.1. Notice that the messages effect can be tested, and in this case it turns out to be both substantial and significant: $F(8,40) = 5.48$, $p < .001$. If messages within categories differ one from another—as the significant F ratio suggests—then average differences among groups of messages will also differ, even if all of the messages come from a single category. In general, when messages-within-categories appears as a significant effect within a replicated categorical comparison design (and also sometimes when it falls short of significance), it is unreasonable to assume that means for message categories are unaffected by the particular messages chosen to represent them.

If the implication of significant message-to-message variability is insufficiently plain, we can approach the issue from a slightly different angle. Note that within the sample of messages as given, there is plenty of reason to believe that the estimate of categorical differences will vary according to the messages observed. If, for example, we selected subsamples of two messages from each category without replacement, the means for the Category A messages could range between 9 and 15, while the means for the Category B messages could range between 12 and 16. In other words, for subsamples of two messages per category, the difference between Category A and Category B could range between a 3-point advantage for Category A and a 7-point advantage for Category B. For subsamples of three messages from each category, the possibilities range from a 1.33-point advantage for Category A to a 5.33-point advantage for Category B. For subsamples of four messages, the possibilities range from no difference to a 3.5-point advantage for Category B. For samples *with replacement* of five messages from each category—something like Efron's (1982) "bootstrap" samples, using messages rather than respondents as the unit of analysis—the possible class-to-class differences range from a 4-point advantage for Category A to a 10-point advantage for Category B. While we will return to this point later for more discussion, its present relevance is in illustrating how variations within a category affect comparisons between categories. If these were real data, we would note the presence of message-to-message variability not as an assumption made by the researcher, but as a fact about the data.

Now, it will be objected by some (and has in fact been argued by Morley, 1988, Wike & Church, 1976, and others) that the fixed-effect analysis is appropriate if we want only to assess a difference *within* the sample of messages at hand, without any particular interest in generalizing to other levels. This sounds doctrinaire, but its plausibility depends upon imprecision of expression. Presumably, what is intended here is an analytic strategy in which the statistical analysis purports only to evaluate the categorical difference for the restricted sample of messages at hand, leaving open the possibility of some form of nonstatistical justification for generalization to a broader set of messages. But the fixed-effect analysis does not satisfy even this limited and conservative purpose. It provides no warrant for believing that the between-categories differences are any greater than would be expected if we were to simply divide the individual messages at hand into random groupings, though it does, of course, give evidence of whether a specific group of concrete messages differs from another specific concrete group of messages. This is a subtle point, but quite important.

Consider: In the example data set appearing in Table 5.1, there are 126 unique ways of dividing the 10 messages into two groups of 5 (twice that many of allocating 5 messages to Category A and 5 messages to Category B). Of the 126 unique ways of dividing the message set in half, just about 25% result in mean differences as great as the difference observed. If one were to sort the 10 messages into groups in a random fashion, without regard for the particular categorization the experimenter had in mind, there would be quite a good chance (better than 25%) of getting mean differences as great as were obtained in the given data set. Whatever value is obtained for the Option B F ratio, how is one to respond to the objection that mere message-to-message variability could easily account for the apparent differences between categories? The treatment of messages as fixed (as recommended by Morley) does not justify a categorical interpretation of the results at all; nor is it reasonable to suggest that a categorical interpretation may be drawn from a significant Option B F ratio, then generalized "nonstatistically" (as was earlier argued by Wike & Church, 1976). If messages within a group differ one from another, then groups of messages—even those drawn from a common population—will also differ one from another, and in the fixed-effect analysis of a replicated categorical comparison, there is no way to establish that the observed difference between one mean and another goes beyond what would be found between any two randomly sorted groups of messages.

Clearly, a significant F ratio for the category effect obtained under Option B does not establish a *categorical* difference, even for the messages actually included in the sample. Such an analysis establishes that two concrete groups of messages each differ from one another, but since any differences between the two concrete groups may reflect nothing more than case-to-case differences occurring even within categories, the observation that the two concrete groups of messages differ does not justify the conclusion that the categories differ. Another way of putting this is to say that under the messages-fixed analysis, the notion of a *message category* becomes superfluous, since all that is really accomplished under such an analysis is a comparison of a particular fixed collection of messages with another fixed collection of messages. Notice, for example, that a conclusion about the difference between the two groups of messages cannot even be assumed to hold for subsamples within the groups.

How does the messages-random analysis deal with the problem of disentangling categorical differences from mere case-to-case differences? Unlike the messages-fixed analysis, the messages-random analysis "discounts" between-groups differences by an amount representing the difference that could be expected simply from message-to-message variability. The variance among the category means is assumed to represent not only categorical differences, but also case-specific variability whose magnitude can be estimated from the case-to-case differences within categories.

To summarize, the choice of whether to treat the replications factor as having fixed or random levels is dependent upon what is assumed about the impact of individual replications on the estimation of the categorical differences. But what is assumed is accountable to the data. Any non-nil main effect for messages within categories creates a presumption that the particular messages chosen for study affect the category means computed over those messages. This presumption rules out the possibility of either ignoring messages as a factor (Option A) or treating the messages as fixed (Option B). By itself, the presumption does not, of course, justify Option C, though it is the basic motivation for Option C or something very like it. Later in the chapter, we will consider objections that have been raised against treating messages as random, and in Chapter 6 we will consider some statistical alternatives that might either solve or avoid these objections.

Analysis of Replicated Treatment Comparison Designs

Consider now the second prototype, messages crossed with treatments. Most experiments with message variables fit this type, except that in the existing literature most of these experiments use only a single kernel message so that there is only one level of the messages factor. A replicated treatments design comes about by gathering a number of kernel messages, and then subjecting each one to the experimental manipulation to produce contrasting versions of each kernel message. These contrasting versions of each kernel message are then presented to independent groups of respondents, so that the respondents within one level of the experimental treatment are divided among message replicates, and the respondents within one level of the messages factor are likewise divided among the experimental treatment conditions.

As with the first prototype, we have available three analytic options: ignore the messages factor, retain the messages factor but treat its levels as fixed, or retain the messages factor and treat its levels as random. All three options are illustrated numerically for the data in Table 5.3.

The unacceptability of the first option is even clearer here than in the categorical comparison design; it will not be discussed further. But Options B and C require consideration.

We begin, as before, with a model of the individual score:

$$X_{ijk} = \mu + \tau_i + \gamma_j + \tau\gamma_{ij} + \epsilon_{ijk}$$

where τ_i is the treatment effect for the ith treatment level; γ_j is the message effect for the jth message; $\tau\gamma_{ij}$, representing the $T \times M$

TABLE 5.3. Three Analytic Options Illustrated Numerically for the Replicated Treatments Design

	Data (n per cell = 10)			
	Treatment 1 cell statistics		Treatment 2 cell statistics	
Message 1	$\overline{X} = 10$	$SS = 36$	$\overline{X} = 13$	$SS = 44$
Message 2	$\overline{X} = 9$	$SS = 44$	$\overline{X} = 11$	$SS = 40$
Message 3	$\overline{X} = 11$	$SS = 44$	$\overline{X} = 13$	$SS = 28$
Message 4	$\overline{X} = 13$	$SS = 42$	$\overline{X} = 12$	$SS = 40$
Message 5	$\overline{X} = 10$	$SS = 40$	$\overline{X} = 9$	$SS = 42$

Analysis: Sums of squares and mean squares

	Option A		Option B		Option C	
Source	SS	MS	SS	MS	SS	MS
Treatment	25	25			25	25
Messages			134	33.5	134	33.5
$M \times T$			70	17.5	70	17.5
Subjects	604	6.16	400	4.44	400	4.44

interaction, can be conceptualized as a correction applied to the treatment effect for the individual message, and ϵ_{ijk} is error, ordinarily conceptualized as the variation contributed by the individual respondent.

The analysis of variance results in a sum of squares and a mean square corresponding to each "source" of variance implied by this model. But computed variances for row means, column means, cell means, and so on, generally "contain" variance due to more than one underlying source. For example, we assume that the variance among the treatment means is due partly to true treatment variance but partly to error variance. And as before, exactly what an observed variance is thought to contain depends on what choice is made concerning the replication factor.

The difference between Options B and C, as before, is not in what sums of squares and mean squares are computed for each effect in the design, but in what is assumed about the composition of these values. The Option B analysis assumes that the particular messages involved in the experiment do not affect the estimation of the treatment effect. (This would be the case, for example, if the effect of the treatment was invariant from message to message. It would also be the case if we defined the effect of interest in terms of those messages and only those messages included in the experiment, but we will disregard this situation, since in the unusual case where it might apply, there will be no controversy over the appropriateness of the Option B analysis.) The Option C analysis recognizes the possibility that differences among treatment levels may appear larger or smaller depending upon the particular messages to which the treatment is applied. The variability in the size of the treatment effect from message to message within the sample is taken as a basis for estimating the sampling error in the estimate of the effect.

Expected mean squares for the second prototype are shown in Table 5.4. As before, the difference between the fixed-effect model and the random-effect model is in whether the treatment mean square is or is not assumed to be afflicted by variance related to the particular messages studied, except that in the messages–crossed design, it is the variability of the treatment effect from message replication to message replication that complicates our ability to estimate the treatment effect (Jackson et al., 1989).

Unless the treatment × message interaction is nil (that is, unless the treatment effect is the same for every message), the differences among the treatment levels must be regarded as partly due to message-related sampling error. To see why, imagine that the average "true" treatment effect is zero, but that the effect of applying the treatment to any one particular message varies around the average of zero, sometimes producing an advantage for one message strategy and sometimes an advantage for its opposite. In any concrete group of messages to which the treatment is applied, there will be some average difference between the contrasted strategies, and the variability of this average is a function of how much variability there is in the treatment from individual message to individual message. When the treatment

TABLE 5.4. Expected Mean Squares for Three Options

Option A (messages ignored)	Treatment	$mn\sigma_\tau^2$		$+\ \sigma_\epsilon^2$
	Respondents/T			σ_ϵ^2
Option B (messages fixed)	Treatment	$mn\sigma_\tau^2$		$+\ \sigma_\epsilon^2$
	Messages		$tn\sigma_\gamma^2$	$+\ \sigma_\epsilon^2$
	$T \times M$		$n\sigma_{\tau\gamma}^2$	$+\ \sigma_\epsilon^2$
	Respondents/ $T \times M$			σ_ϵ^2
Option C (messages random)	Treatment	$mn\sigma_\tau^2$	$+\ n\sigma_{\tau\gamma}^2$	$+\ \sigma_\epsilon^2$
	Messages		$tn\sigma_\gamma^2$	$+\ \sigma_\epsilon^2$
	$T \times M$		$n\sigma_{\tau\gamma}^2$	$+\ \sigma_\epsilon^2$
	Respondents/ $T \times M$			σ_ϵ^2

Note: t is the number of treatments, m is the number of message replications, and n is the number of respondents per cell.

effect must be presumed to vary from one individual message to another (as would have to be presumed if the treatment × message interaction were significant), it must also be presumed that the estimate of the treatment effect contains some unwanted message-related variance.

Consider the example data set in Table 5.3. We can see that the estimate of the treatment effect does in fact depend on the particular messages chosen for study, just as we could see that the estimate of the categorical effect in Table 5.1 depended on the particular messages chosen for study, by examining the results under various sorts of resamplings. If we draw any sort of subsamples from the messages actually included in the experiment (for the moment keeping audiences intact), we can see that the experimental outcomes are not uniform, but variable. For three of the messages, Treatment 2 appears better than Treatment 1; for the fourth and fifth, Treatment 1 appears better than Treatment 2. Now these observations are not free from the ordinary sort of sampling error we associate with human respondents, but let us ignore that complexity for the moment. Consider what would happen to our assessment of the treatment effect if we were to eliminate any one of the five messages (and, of course, also the several respondents responding to the eliminated message), basing our analysis on the remaining four. We might think of this as the result of having stopped with four replications. Depending on which message is eliminated, the advantage of Treatment 2 over Treatment 1 could range from 0.5 units to 1.5 units. The variability of estimates computed over smaller samples, say two or three messages at a time instead of four at a time, is of course greater. This is partly, but not wholly, a consequence of the gain or loss of the respondents assigned to each message.

The sensitivity of the treatment effect estimate to the sample is evident within the sample itself. The vulnerability of the estimate of the treatment effect to message-related sampling error is virtually unarguable whenever the treatment × message interaction is significant, and also presumable whenever the treatment × message mean square is substantially greater than the within-groups mean square (even if not significant). Evident variability within a sample is very good grounds for assuming that there will be variability from one sample to another, and more importantly for our purposes, it is very good grounds for assuming that any one sample will produce an estimate that deviates to some extent from the underlying "true" value we wish to estimate. Observed treatment differences must be "discounted" for this kind of variability.

As with the first prototype, the major statistical consequence of treating messages as random is seen in the test of the treatment main effect; in this prototype, the test does not use the respondents-within-groups mean square as the error term, but instead uses the treatment × message interaction mean square: not the standard fixed-model test, $F = MS_T/MS_{P/TM}$, but the mixed-model test $F = MS_T/MS_{T \times M}$. (The remaining option, ignoring the messages replication factor, leads to a redefinition of the within-groups variance as deviations of individual responses from treatment means, creating two forms of nonindependence.)

As in the analysis of the replicated categorical comparison, the three analytic options yield quite different F ratios for the main effect of interest:

Option A (replications ignored): $F(1,98) = 4.058$, $p = .047$.
Option B (replications fixed): $F(1,90) = 5.625$, $p = .02$.
Option C (replications random): $F(1,4) = 1.429$, $p = .298$.

It is interesting to notice that the Option C F ratio fits better with a common-sense interpretation of the data than do the Option A and B F ratios. Both the Option A F ratio and the Option B F ratio suggest a reliable difference between the two treatments, when it is clear from Table 5.3 that the difference is quite unreliable. The advantage of Treatment 2 over Treatment 1 is not at all consistent, and in fact it is disadvantageous in two of the five cases. The significant Option B F ratio warrants an expectation that the same ten messages presented to 100 new respondents will show an advantage for the Treatment 2 versions; but it does not warrant an expectation that this effect will hold even for subsets of the original messages, much less for new messages to which the treatment might be applied.

The Option C F ratio yields a null result, and that is about what common sense tells us we have. In the five cases examined, three show an advantage for Treatment 2, and two show an advantage for Treatment 1. There is no way to tell from this set of cases whether there is any systematic advantage for one treatment or the other. The only conclusion that can be drawn is that to evaluate the effect, given how variable it appears to be, a great many individual messages should be examined.

But could anything like this occur in real (as opposed to contrived) data? Consider the experiment recently reported by Burgoon, Hall, and Pfau (1991), a test of the effectiveness of inoculation messages in making audience members resistant to subsequent attack messages.

The treatment variable, inoculation, had two levels: A respondent either received an inoculation message, or not, prior to hearing an "attack" message. Those receiving the inoculation may be considered the treatment group, and those not receiving it may be considered a control group. There were six replications of the basic treatment/control comparison, each using independent sets of inoculation and attack messages. Altogether, there were 12 groups figuring in the test of the inoculation effect: two treatment levels crossed with six replications. The mean attitude scores taken after presentation of the attack messages are summarized in Table 5.5 below (from Burgoon et al., Table 2).

Burgoon et al. conducted one-tailed tests of the inoculation effect, using all three of the analytic options discussed above. For purposes of illustration, we will simplify the analysis by positing equal cell sizes of 67 per group, for a total N of 804. (There were in fact 806 respondents, divided unevenly among the 12 groups, but this adds complexities irrelevant to our present concerns.) We will also stipulate that the total variance in the dependent measure is 15,729.653, a value estimated from values of F ratios given in the report. It should be noted that the results obtained with these stipulations will differ slightly from the actual results, but they are nevertheless useful in illustrating the differences among the three analytic options, and they should approximate the results of unweighted means analysis of variance (with the closeness of the approximation dependent on the unevenness in the cell sizes).

The Option A analysis partitions the total sum of squares into two sources, the treatment and the respondents within treatments, as shown in the ANOVA summary table below. The treatment F ratio, computed as a ratio of mean squares for treatment and respondents

TABLE 5.5. Treatment-by-Replication Cell Means

Message set	Control	Inoculation
1	23.04	20.90
2	25.00	23.98
3	24.82	23.84
4	22.57	22.00
5	27.05	27.53
6	23.34	24.25
Overall	24.31	23.75

Note. Data are from Burgoon et al. (1991).

within treatments, is significant at the .05 level, considering the test to be one-tailed.

	SS	df	MS	$F^{[A]}$
Treatment	61.54	1	61.54	3.15
Within treatments	15,668.11	803	19.54	

The Option B and Option C analyses partition the total sums of squares into four sources, as shown below. But the two analyses test the treatment effect differently. When messages are treated as fixed, the F for the treatment uses the respondents-within-groups mean square as the denominator, yielding a value of 3.745. This value, like the Option A result, is significant at the .05 level, considering the test to be one-tailed. When messages are treated as random, the F for the treatment uses the treatment $\times$ message interaction as the error term, yielding a value of 1.499. This value is nonsignificant, regardless of whether the test is considered one-tailed or two-tailed.

	SS	df	MS	$F^{[B]}$	$F^{[C]}$
Treatment	61.54	1	61.54	3.745	1.499
Messages	2,448.61	5	489.72		
$T \times M$	205.22	5	41.04		
Within groups	13,014.28	792	16.43		

In the Burgoon et al. study, the choice of analytic option makes a considerable difference to what we conclude about the effects of inoculation. On the Option A and Option B analyses, the inoculation effect is judged to be significant, while on the Option C analysis, it is not. Such a pattern will not always occur, but the point to be taken is that these forms of analysis differ, and the choice among them should be based on which *form* of analysis can be given the best defense, not on which actual F ratio gives the most favorable result.

In general, when a replicated treatments design is used, the Option B and Option C F ratios will differ to the extent that the treatment effect varies from replication to replication, that is, to the extent that treatments interact with messages. Note that the Option C F ratio could be expressed as a ratio of two Option B F ratios, the F for the treatment effect divided by the F for the interaction. When the F for the interaction is larger than 1, the Option C F ratio will necessarily be smaller than the Option B F ratio.

General Implications of Treating Messages as Random

Inspection of both Table 5.1 and Table 5.3 shows that the expected mean square for the messages error term includes not only a variance component representing the message effect, but also a variance component representing the respondents effect. The decision to test treatment effects against the treatment × message interaction (or, in the first prototype, to test a categorical difference against the differences among cases within categories) is not a decision to ignore variability due to respondents.[2]

For both prototypes, it should be clear that the choice of whether to treat replications as fixed or as random is consequential primarily in determining the statistical test for categorical differences or treatment effects. Obviously, a test conducted treating messages as fixed answers a different question than a test conducted treating messages as random. There is a subtle but genuine difference between asking whether two groups of concrete objects differ from one another and asking whether two sets of objects differ *as classes* from one another; the fixed-effect analysis addresses the first question and the random-effect analysis the second.

Unless the contrast of interest is wholly unaffected by which particular messages are studied, the treatment of messages as fixed precludes any generic conclusion about the differences between one message category and another or about the effect of a message treatment. The common belief that treating replications as fixed simply limits generalizability of the generic conclusion to the particular replications studied is incorrect, for even within the particular replication set studied, the fixed-effect analysis offers no basis for judging whether apparent between-group differences are anything more than accumulated between-case differences. This line of reasoning suggests that most of the time messages should be treated as a random factor, since it is not ordinarily reasonable to suppose that members of a message category are entirely uniform with respect to the dependent variable or that a message treatment will have entirely uniform effects across its domain of applicability.

OBJECTIONS TO TREATING MESSAGES AS RANDOM

So far we have established that replications included in any design cannot simply be ignored, and that to treat them as fixed is to defeat the purpose of including them. If messages are included as replications in order to take into account message-related variability of effect, only one of the three statistical alternatives described above offers any semblance of consistency with the design objectives, and that is to treat the replications as random. This does not, of course, establish the appropriateness and desirability of the random-effect analysis, but only its superiority over the two alternatives so far considered.

A great deal has been written (especially in the psycholinguistics research literature) about the propriety of treating replications as random and about the practical disadvantages of doing so. Following the publication of Clark's (1973) essay on "the language-as-fixed-effect fallacy," numerous researchers and methodologists involved themselves in debate over how best to deal with language replications (typically words or sentences) included in experiments. Some of the disputed issues have since been resolved through empirical investigations of the properties of certain statistics, but others remain as lively concerns, especially among communication researchers, for whom the message stimuli of interest are not typically words and sentences, but speeches and essays.

The first of these current controversies is the propriety, in principle, of treating replications selected nonrandomly as levels of a random factor. This is a theoretical issue, concerned with the justifiability of a statistical procedure within a substantive research context. The second controversy to be considered is the practical issue of whether analysis of the sort I have advocated will offer sufficient power for the purposes of communication researchers.

The "Foundationalist" Critique: Random Means Random

A common objection to treating messages as random is that messages cannot be sampled at random, and therefore should not be treated as random in statistical analysis. The slogan "random means random" comes from the title of one of several critical responses to Clark's "language-as-fixed-effect fallacy" (Cohen, 1976; see also Morley, 1988; Keppel, 1976; Wike & Church, 1976). I will call this the "foundationalist" critique, because its thrust is to challenge the mathematical foundations of the analytic strategy. It is a serious argument with extremely wide-ranging implications, not only for experimentation with messages, but also for all sorts of research involving human respondents selected nonrandomly.

Critics of Clark's proposal that language stimuli be treated as random effects in psycholinguistic research argued that statistical tests of the difference between two language categories rest on an assumption that cases within each category are random samples of all possible cases. This assumption, they argued, is central to the defense of the sample variance as a basis for estimating population variance, and hence for estimation of standard error. Where cases have been chosen systematically or arbitrarily, Clark's critics argued, they should be treated as fixed effects. If correct, this argument would rule out treating most message replication factors as random, since it is not possible to sample most language and message categories at random.

Clark (1976) responded that random sampling is indeed desirable, but that, even in the absence of random sampling, materials chosen as representatives of a category or as replications of a treatment cannot be treated as fixed, for to do so is to assume that the particular materials chosen for the study make no contribution to the variability in the observed differences or effects. In the discussion that has followed, the emerging consensus seems to be that treating replications as random is less than perfectly justified, but much more appropriate than the alternatives (see Richter & Seay, 1987; Santa et al., 1979; Wickens & Keppel, 1983).

Examining the arguments on both sides of this issue, what stands out most is the absence of detailed attention to the nature of statistical inference or the purposes of statistical testing. The association of statistical tests with the task of "generalizing" is one source of difficulty, for generalization in the sense of extrapolation from sample to population is not what significance tests are normally expected to accomplish within experiments. On the contrary, inferential statistics conducted on experimental outcomes ordinarily do not involve an extrapolation from the sample to some concrete population but from the observations to some abstract null-hypothesis distribution of outcomes. This null-hypothesis distribution is built up from the data themselves and what we choose to assume about the effect to be tested.

Consider the role of the significance test for category differences within a replicated categorical comparison. The task of the test is to decide whether the observations do or do not justify a conclusion that the several categories differ from one another "in principle." Background to this decision is the manifest dependency of the category mean on the specific members chosen to represent it and on the specific people chosen to respond to these members. When all of the members of the category are very uniform in value, and when all of the individual respondents give uniform evaluations, the category mean may be assumed to be relatively unaffected by which members of the category are evaluated or which people do the evaluating. But when the members of the category are highly variable in value or when the individual respondents give highly variable evaluations, it is to be assumed that category means will fluctuate depending on message sample and re-spondent sample. The question to be answered by the significance test may be phrased as follows: Given the unsystematic variability observed in the sample (among messages within categories and among people within groups), would category differences of the size observed be likely to come about in the absence of true category differences?

Thinking about the task of the significance test in this way, a null-hypothesis distribution of outcomes can be generated without recourse to any concrete population of messages or people. The null-hypothesis distribution assumes that category means are equal in prin-ciple but that both respondents and messages contribute stipulated amounts of variance to the means, with these stipulated amounts being drawn from the observed variance among respondents within groups and among messages within categories. We can think about the null hypothesis as positing an imaginary population "as variable as" the sample, but with no true categorical differences, for the sole purpose of deciding whether differences among category means such as those observed in the sample can be accounted for as the normal, expectable consequence of case-to-case or person-to-person variation. Similar reasoning can be reconstructed for the case of evaluating treat-ment effects.

Another way to look at the significance test is as part of an argument for the claim that several categories or several treatments differ. When a researcher puts forward a claim about the difference between two message classes or the effect of a message treatment, the burden of proof associated with the claim includes some answer to the counterclaim that the differences observed are only such as would be expected as a consequence of case-to-case and person-to-person variation. This counterclaim (that there are no true category or treatment differences, but only unsystematic sources of variances producing apparent differences) takes the observable variation from case to case and from person to person as its starting point, and so must any rebuttal to it. To show that the differences observed are not the sort of differences that would be expectable simply because of case-to-case and person-to-person variation, the researcher must compare the obtained result with an abstract null-hypothesis distribution of outcomes in which case-to-case and person-to-person variations are the only contributions to observed differences among categories or treatments.

When a categorical comparison is at issue, the null hypothesis is most plausible when the difference between two category means is small relative to the differences among individual messages within categories, and it is least plausible when the difference between the means is large relative to the differences among individual messages. When a treatment comparison is at issue, the null hypothesis is most plausible when the average treatment effect is small relative to the variability in effect from message to message and least plausible when the treatment effect is large relative to the variability in effect. That is, *consistency of effect from message to message is important in evaluating the averaged effect.*

More generally, the null hypothesis gains plausibility as we show that the sort of difference observed could easily arise in a sample of the size we have observed from a null-hypothesis population envisioned as having a true difference of 0 and a variance about like that observed in the sample. A significant Option C F ratio for a categorical difference or treatment effect defeats the argument that differences can be accounted for in terms of unsystematic variance due to messages and respondents, by showing that a difference of the sort observed would be unlikely to occur in an arbitrary sample from the null-hypothesis population.

The foundationalist critique of treating messages as random rests on a conviction that there is no way to justify any inference about the distribution of a treatment mean or category mean without assuming that the observations have been chosen at random from the relevant population. The usual way, as described in standard textbook treatments of statistical inference, is to proceed in a top-down fashion, setting up hypothetical conditions under which we would be able to infer properties of the population's distribution from observation of a sample. These hypothetical conditions may involve assumptions about the form of the distribution (its normality) and about the manner in which the sample has been drawn (its randomness), and their role is to allow for deductions about the distributions of sample statistics.

But this usual way of proceeding is not the only conceivable way of proceeding. If we find it inconvenient or inappropriate to make one set of assumptions about the nature of the population or the nature of the sample, there is nothing to prevent us from searching for other starting points. Instead of assuming that the sample is a random selection from a predefined population, we might treat a given sample of independently selected replications as definitive of a model population that exists only as an abstraction. To this model population we attribute the manifest variability among individual cases observed in the sample, and we use this attribution in a provisional way to assess the evidence in favor of a categorical difference or a treatment effect, as against the null hypothesis that there are no systematic differences beyond the manifest (but so far unanalyzed) case-to-case differences.

A point worth noting is that different foundations do not necessarily lead to different procedures, though they probably lead to somewhat different interpretations. The manner in which we calculate the "standard error of the mean" does not, for example, require the assumption of normality, nor does it depend on any possibility of defining a population in advance and drawing from it a "random sample" in the ordinary sense (Efron, 1982). Likewise, we can scrap one or more of the well-known "assumptions of the F test" and arrive at the same procedures from other assumptions; instead of taking the sample as a random selection from the population, and hence a basis for unbiased estimation, we jump directly to the stipulation of a model population in which the cases are as variable as the cases in the sample. Textbook lists of assumptions of the F test are sufficient to justify a certain interpretation of the results of the F test (sometimes termed a "frequentist" interpretation), but it is by no means clear that any particular list is *necessary* to derive either the F distribution or the important conclusion that the F ratio will have an F distribution when the null hypothesis is true. Nor is the sort of interpretation underwritten by these assumptions self-evidently useful.

This brief discussion aims only to suggest that significance tests serve, argumentatively, as measures of the plausibility of a claim, as against a "presumption of nullity." A significant F test for differences between two categories is a plausible argument for the existence of categorical differences that go beyond mere case-to-case differences. A demonstration that categorical effects exceed what might be expected based on what we know of case-to-case differences (or that treatment effects exceed what might be explained in terms of case-to-case variability around a mean of 0) changes the argumentative context in an interesting way. In argumentation theory, it would be said that such a demonstration shifts the presumption from the null claim to the claim of categorical differences. What this means is that further challenges to the claim of categorical difference—objections based, say, on the nature of the sample—require substantiation. To sustain the null claim once it has been shown that differences between means exceed what would be expected based on case-to-case variability, it would be necessary to give reason to believe that the samples give a systematically distorted picture of the relationship between the two categories. It would be necessary, for example, to show that the sampling procedure was biased, or that the cases were drawn from a pool constrained in some important way. A general refusal to take the sample variance as an unbiased estimate of the population variance will not justify rejection of claims about how likely a result would be within a population as variable as the sample.

The foundationalist critique of treating messages (and other replications, including human respondents) as random rests on an unexamined assumption that a statistical procedure can only be used to do one sort of argumentative task and can only be justified in one way. A contrary position is suggested here: Statistical procedures have situated argumentative tasks that may require special, situated justifications and special, situated interpretations. Clearly, there are limits on what one may argue from a significant F ratio computed for comparisons between arbitrarily selected samples of two different sorts of objects. However, within these limits there is useful argumentative work to be done. This is what the foundationalist critics have failed to see.

Is it possible for a procedure to be "useful" without being "justified" in the foundationalist sense? Consider the case at issue: the usefulness of statistical tests treating messages as random. The claims to be contrasted are on the one side that differences between two comparison groups of messages represent some sort of systematic difference between the groups, and on the other side that differences between the two groups represent only the sort of difference that might result from the unsystematic variability one might observe from any one message to another. Both of these claims share some substantive assumptions: that the individual messages vary one from another for unknown reasons, and that averages taken over groups of messages vary to some extent as a consequence of this uncontrolled variation. A *useful* procedure can be constructed from this shared set of substantive assumptions, and even if the shared assumptions cannot themselves be "justified," the procedure might build a very convincing case against one or the other of the contrasting claims.

If statistical analysis is seen as guided by specific questions to be answered and specific claims to be defended, the foundationalist critique loses much of its initial plausibility. The possibility that apparent category differences are ungenuine can only be answered by comparing the magnitude of category differences with what would be expected from case differences alone; and this is precisely what is accomplished by treating messages as random. The issue of whether to treat replications as fixed or random has been discussed extremely thoroughly in the psycholinguistics literature, as noted earlier, and the consensus position now appears to be (as Cornfield & Tukey argued in 1956) that "sampled" factors (here termed replications) should uniformly be treated as random, regardless of whether the materials sampled are selected randomly or arbitrarily (see, for example, Wickens & Keppel, 1983, or Richter & Seay, 1987). The position taken here is more extreme only in rejecting any suggestion that the analysis would be better "justified" if messages were in fact drawn at random from some population of possibilities. Within a conscientiously carried-out view of method as argumentative, a sufficient "justification" for a statistical procedure is that it allows us to reason from the premises of a meaningful null hypothesis to either a rejection of (or a recognizable failure to reject) that null hypothesis.

Statistical Power

A second objection to treatment of message replications as random —more practical than theoretical—is that doing so will lead to significance tests with unacceptably low power. When message replications are treated as levels of a random factor, nested under categories or crossed with experimental treatments, the power to detect categorical or treatment effects is constrained by the number of message replications (rather than simply by the number of human respondents). Although increasing the number of respondents in a multiple-message design does increase power to detect treatment effects, this increase is constrained by the number of message replications. This has been widely discussed as a possible objection to treating messages as random (see, e.g., Hunter et al., 1989; Morley, 1988).

As several authors have noted, the limitations on power associated with treatment of messages as a random factor do not constitute a valid basis for preferring a treatment of messages as fixed (e.g., Wickens & Keppel, 1983). When messages are treated as fixed, the hypothesis tested is different from the hypothesis we need to test in order to make a case for or against a claim. Specifically, when messages are treated as fixed, we test the hypothesis that responses to a fixed, concrete group of messages differ from responses to another fixed, concrete group of messages, when what is wanted is a test of whether a category differs from a category.

In a limited empirical investigation of power in replicated treatment comparisons, Dale Brashers and I came to several general conclusions (Jackson & Brashers, 1990). First, power to detect any treatment effect depends not only on the size of the message sample, but also on the amount of variability in the treatment effect from message to message. Second, with a fixed number of human respondents, power to detect treatment effects increases with an increase in the number of message replications; this is true even when the consequence is a very small number of respondents responding to each individual message. Third, increases in the power to detect treatment effects trades off against power to detect treatment × message interactions; in other words, when message replications are added to a design, the power to test the treatment main effect increases while the power to test the treatment × message interaction declines (except for very small numbers of messages). Nevertheless, if the principal purpose of an experiment is to evaluate a treatment effect, then it is advisable to incorporate as many message replications as possible. Fourth, and perhaps most important for the actual conduct of research, power to detect treatment effects is inadequate for designs using very small numbers of replications, say two or three.

Now, message samples are harder to generate than human samples, since we are often in a position to recruit 100 human participants as easily as 10, while messages have to be located, written, edited, and prepared for use one at a time. Setting out with a certain level of power in mind and generating enough message replications to reach that level of power given whatever might be assumed about average effect size and variability of effect size is probably not practical. But it is clear that the researcher should take seriously the size of the message sample and should make some effort to adjust the size of the message sample to the assumed variability of the effect.

Because power depends on how variable message effects are, there can be no reasonable rule of thumb for how many message replications to include, but the number required to achieve adequate power may be smaller than many seem to think. For example, in persuasion research, many effects are variable enough to require *some* replications, but variable within a narrow enough range to permit reasonable power with about ten replications. Without prior knowledge of how the effects of interest vary from message to message, an experimenter would be safer including a larger number of replications.

The most direct way of boosting power to detect treatment effects or categorical effects is to generate more messages. (Some practical strategies for doing so are discussed in Chapter 7.) The most direct way to avoid the trade-off between power to detect treatment effects and power to detect message-by-treatment interactions is to increase the number of respondents. With fixed resources of either type, it may still be possible to boost power, by introducing classification variables to reduce unexplained message-to-message variability. This procedure is analogous to "subsetting" of studies in meta-analysis; in addition to increasing the power to detect a treatment effect, it can yield substantively interesting moderators of the effect.

SUMMARY

In this chapter we have considered three methods for the analysis of experiments with message replications. Neither ignoring messages nor treating them as fixed is acceptable as a general policy. Treating messages as random is consistent with the stance usually taken toward replications in experiments and with the argumentative work that the replications are expected to do. We have considered two objections to treating messages as random in the statistical analysis of a replicated experiment. The first objection charges that such an analysis is invalid because it violates certain assumptions required for valid interpretation of the result. Such an objection rests on an inaccurate understanding of the goals of the analysis and an overly simplified conception of how one might argue from its results. The second objection charges that such an analysis lacks power as compared with its alternatives. This objection rests on the false notion that the alternatives test the same hypothesis; to compare the power of a mixed-model analysis of variance with a fixed-model analysis of the same observations is bogus.

Treating messages as a random factor will obviously give rise to problems not yet solved within the social sciences. However, even if such problems prove insoluble, they will not justify treating messages as fixed or ignoring them altogether in the analysis. Hence, it is important to give some thought to other directions that might be taken in the analysis of replicated experiments. This is the task of the next chapter.

SIX

Alternative Statistical Procedures

Chapter 5 describes one way of attacking the statistical problems that arise from the incorporation of message replications into experiments on message effects. The general intent of Chapter 5 is to show that it will normally be possible and defensible to evaluate message effects using familiar analysis-of-variance procedures. For various sorts of reasons, some logical and some merely practical, such an approach may not be usable in some cases. When that is so, we may decline to analyze the experiment as a mixed-model analysis of variance, but then we will have to find some other way of accomplishing the same thing. We will need functional substitutes for this form of analysis— that is, alternative procedures for meeting the same burden of proof—whenever we find we cannot use the statistical tests described in earlier chapters. For example, if we come up against barriers to including adequate numbers of messages in an experiment or objections to treating messages as random, we may be forced to resort to some different design-and-analysis strategy, but each alternative strategy must provide some sort of response to the issues raised in Chapter 2: Each alternative must offer some way of answering the various threats to validity of causal claims about messages. The purpose of this chapter is to consider some of the alternatives that have been proposed or might be proposed.

META-ANALYSIS AS A SUBSTITUTE FOR REPLICATED DESIGNS

Several critics of the replicated experiment have proposed "meta-analysis" of large bodies of unreplicated experiments as an alternative to the overall design-and-analysis strategy described in this book. Proposals of this sort appear, for example, in Morley (1988) and in Hunter et al. (1989). Generally, proponents of meta-analysis as a substitute for replicated experiments restrict their attention to treatment comparisons (rather than categorical comparisons), reasoning that treatment comparisons are free from confounding and that the task of meta-analysis is simply to assess average treatment effects, taking into account the variability of these effects from one study to another.

This proposal—as it has been put forward to date—involves not merely a substitution of one set of statistics for another, but a substitution of an entire design strategy for another. The proposal is an effort to avoid replicated experiments entirely, not a strategy for *analyzing* replicated experiments. Nevertheless, it is worthy of consideration in this chapter for two reasons: The first is that meta-analysis directs attention to some important features of inference and generalization, and the second is that its procedures can be applied *within* replicated experiments, sometimes to good effect. In this section, we will explore the possibility of using meta-analysis of large bodies of unreplicated experiments to substitute for replicated experiments entirely, and in the next we will consider the question of whether meta-analysis statistics might substitute for analysis of variance within replicated experiments.

Meta-analysis refers to any of a number of techniques for quantitative integration of the results of many individual studies of the same effect. Several competing approaches have been proposed, for example by Glass, McGaw, and Smith (1981), Hedges and Olkin (1985), and Hunter, Schmidt, and Jackson (1982). The common features in these approaches are a reliance on effect-size measurement as a tool for the summary of individual findings and a commitment to the analysis of study-to-study variability in these effect-size measurements. In other respects, the various approaches differ both in theory and in application.

Most meta-analyses of message effects research have used the Hunter, Schmidt, and Jackson approach. Perhaps the most distinctive feature of this approach (as compared, say, with the approach of Glass et al.), is the emphasis on artifact as a source of study-to-study variability. The basic premise is that the estimate of a treatment effect (or other relationship) will vary from study to study, even in the absence of any systematic difference in the nature of the underlying effect, as a result of such things as sampling error, measurement unreliability, restriction of range, and other artifacts. (From a certain point of view, the particular message to which a treatment is applied can also be considered an artifactual source of variance, though so far it has not been common to do so.)

When variability from study to study cannot be adequately explained in terms of these artifactual sources of variance, meta-analysis proceeds to a search for nonartifactual sources of variance, conceptualized substantively as "moderators" of an effect. Moderators, in the message effects literature, might take the form of audience characteristics, topic characteristics, source characteristics, or any other feature of the communication process that might alter the effect of a given message variable. So, for example, in meta-analysis of the research literature dealing with effectiveness of varying fear appeals, Boster and Mongeau (1984) identified audience age as a moderator of the effect: Older audiences are more responsive to variations in fear level than are younger audiences.

Meta-analysis is normally used to make sense of large bodies of existing studies on a common topic. In fact, it is rather pointless unless there are available many independent estimates of the same effect. In the message effects research literature, many different topics have generated bodies of research large enough to make meta-analysis worthwhile. For example, there are over 50 experimental studies of the relative effectiveness of different levels of fear appeal, a similar number on the relative effectiveness of one-sided and two-sided argumentation, dozens on the effectiveness of foot-in-the-door and door-in-the-face persuasive techniques, and so on for many other topics. In some respects, a meta-analysis of a large number of unreplicated experiments is structurally similar to a primary analysis of a single, large, replicated experiment. Within a large number of unreplicated treatment comparisons, one will expect to find the same independent variable manipulated within the context of a large number of different kernel messages; in this respect, the body of studies will contain the same sort of materials as a single large replicated design. Let us consider some of the dissimilarities, however.

One dissimilarity between a meta-analysis of, say, 20 unreplicated experiments and a primary analysis of a single experiment with 20 replications is that any large body of independently conducted experiments will contain a great many incidental variations from message to message not likely to be found within an individual study. For example, 20 different studies will probably not use a common dependent variable; some will measure attitude toward a position advocated in the experimental messages, others will measure judgments of the credibility of the source, others will measure actual behavioral compliance with the message recommendations, and so on. Likewise, the studies will differ in (human) sample characteristics; some will use midwestern college students, others will use Chinese grade school children, and so on. And the studies are likely to differ in design (e.g., independent groups versus repeated measures, posttest-only versus pretest–posttest), and in substantive features of the communication situation involving control of source and context features. This diversity of method is clearly advantageous in many research situations, since it creates a stronger basis for generalization than would a single study—however large—conducted under a single set of particular circumstances. But in the message effects research, where each individual message is studied in a different combination of circumstances, it has the disadvantage of entangling variation in the treatment effect from message to message, with variation in the treatment effect from one set of experimental conditions to another.[1]

Another dissimilarity between a meta-analysis of 20 unreplicated experiments and a primary analysis of a single experiment with 20 replications is that the 20 separate studies will be related to one another in complicated ways. Later studies will build on earlier studies, sometimes repeating experimental messages so as to try to pin down an effect. When this happens, the separate studies do not yield independent estimates of the treatment effect. Likewise, a series of studies is likely to exhibit some sort of conceptual or empirical progression, with the consequence that the 20 replications will not normally be uniform in design, and it is of course also possible that the 20 replications will address a common question in only the loosest sense (see Chow, 1987, for more general discussion of this point).

Suppose we have a large body of experiments on the effect of language intensity, and we wish to meta-analyze the results. A line of research like this will always have some sort of history that will play a part in how the empirical work unfolds. Imagine that the first of the studies shows a significant benefit for increasing the language intensity of a message. Then the second study in the series might add a manipulation of a speaker variable or a context variable so as to build a more differentiated picture of the conditions under which intense language increases persuasiveness. Or the second study might partition the respondents into more homogeneous groups (such as those favorable and unfavorable to the speaker's thesis). This means that the results of the individual studies will not be interchangeable estimates of a common effect in the same sense that results for messages within a study are interchangeable estimates of a common effect. Extra manipulations mean that the effect measured differs subtly from study to study: Adding, say, a credibility manipulation to the basic intensity manipulation means that the study now measures not the effect of the intensity manipulation but its effect in combination with another manipulation. Extra partitions mean that the effect is measured in terms of different units. The effect-size measures commonly used in meta-analysis depend on the within-groups standard deviation as a unit of measure, and this in turn depends on what other factors are included in a design. When studies differ one from another in the number and kind of manipulations and partitions, they lack the comparability present within an equal number of replications handled in parallel. This is clearly disadvantageous, insofar as the objective is estimation of a specific effect. A meta-analyst attentive to these complexities may or may not be able to successfully resolve them, depending on strictly contingent facts like the adequacy of the statistical reporting of the original studies and the availability of sufficient numbers of studies to permit more fine-grained analysis.

Yet another dissimilarity between meta-analysis of 20 unreplicated experiments and primary analysis of a single replicated experiment is in the availability of evidence. Meta-analysts can only work with studies that are recoverable, and then only with studies whose results are codable with respect to the research question. In a replicated experiment, every message incorporated in the design is available to the researcher, regardless of how things "turned out." In a meta-analysis, the researcher must be concerned with whether messages that turned out badly have been suppressed, and with the less adequate reporting of nonsignificant results that is common in the social science literature. This too is clearly disadvantageous.

The discussion so far has pointed to three dissimilarities between meta-analysis of unreplicated experiments and primary analysis of replicated experiments: Large bodies of unreplicated experiments, as compared with a single large replicated experiment (1) hold fewer conditions constant from one message to another; (2) are more likely to vary from message to message in exactly what effect is estimated and less likely to use a consistent standardization basis; (3) are less likely to make available for inspection every message to which the treatment has been applied. On the whole, these differences point to substantial practical disadvantages associated with conducting unreplicated experiments and relying on meta-analysis for combination of results from many such studies. In setting out to research a new question about message effects, it would not make sense to do one unreplicated experiment at a time, hoping for the accumulation of enough usable studies to permit meta-analysis.

This is of course no criticism of meta-analysis, but only of the suggestion that the development of meta-analysis obviates the need for effective primary-level design and analysis. As noted above, a large body of independently produced studies on the same question will offer evidence of generalizability not usually present in any one study. But the opportunities presented by meta-analysis are improved, not worsened, by improvements at the level of primary design and analysis. A meta-analysis done on 20 replicated experiments can hardly be thought inferior to a meta-analysis done on 20 unreplicated experiments. And there is no incompatibility between the use of replicated experiments at the level of primary research and the use of meta-analysis to combine and compare their results at the secondary level.[2]

There is yet another dissimilarity to be considered, and that is in the statistics themselves. This dissimilarity can be treated separately, because it has nothing to do with whether the statistics are computed over a large number of independent experiments or over a large number of replications within a single large experiment (Jackson, 1991). The central issue of interest in the next section is whether meta-analysis statistics, applied *within* a replicated experiment, are a useful alternative to the familiar analysis of variance statistics described in Chapters 3–5.

META-ANALYSIS STATISTICS AS A SUBSTITUTE FOR ANALYSIS OF VARIANCE

As noted earlier, a replicated experiment, in which the same treatment comparison is made multiple times with different materials, is structurally identical to a set of independently conducted unreplicated treatment comparisons. This structural similarity makes it very easy to apply meta-analysis procedures and statistics within replicated experiments, as in an experiment recently reported by Allen et al. (1990). In the Allen et al. experiment, an argument-sidedness manipulation was applied to 17 independent message replications, to produce the sort of design that might give rise to a mixed-model analysis of variance. However, because the 17 independent replications also involved different forms of measurement for the dependent variable, the results were meta-analyzed instead.[3] The main question we will want to address in this section is whether meta-analysis statistics offer any general superiority over analysis of variance for the analysis of replicated experiments—or any escape from the difficult choices they present.

Let us assume that we have at hand a number of identical treatment comparisons, each conducted over a single message replication. We will assume further (for simplicity) that the treatment variable has just two levels, and that the cell sizes are all equal. In the language of Chapter 5, what we have is a t (treatments) × m (replications) design with n observations per cell. If we are considering the possibility of meta-analyzing the study instead of conducting an analysis of variance, it would be useful to know how meta-analysis might compare with analysis of variance performed on the same observations.

Meta-analysis begins with summarization of each independent result, preferably in the form of an effect-size estimate. Our replicated experiment contains m independent estimates of the size of the treatment effect, so we begin by computing a measure of the treatment effect for each replication. Because independent investigations of an effect need not (and usually *do* not) use the same form of measurement for the dependent variable, a standardized effect-size measure is necessary. Two standardized effect-size measures are in common use in communication and related fields: the standardized mean difference d, and the correlation coefficient r.

The standardized mean difference d is simply the difference between two group means (say, between a treatment-group mean and a control-group mean or between two treatment means) divided by the within-group standard deviation(see Cohen, 1977). The difference between two groups is expressed, for each individual experiment, as so many standard deviations. Alternatively, the effect-size can be described in terms of the correlation r between the independent variable and the dependent variable. The two measures are intertranslatable, and there seems to be no clear reason for preferring one over the other.[4] In the discussion that follows, we will use d, because it has particularly transparent connections to the analysis of variance procedures discussed in Chapter 5.

To meta-analyze the results of m independent experiments, we begin by computing an estimate of the size of the treatment effect for each replication. We will consider two alternative forms of d available when the independent estimates come from a common experiment. Let us define s_j as the within-groups standard deviation for the jth replication, and s as the pooled within-groups standard deviation (or the square root of MS_{wg} for the entire t × m layout). Then if $\overline{X}_{ij}$ is the mean response to the ith treatment for the jth replication, we can define the standardized mean difference between Treatment 1 and Treatment 2 as either

$$d_j = (\overline{X}_{2j} - \overline{X}_{1j})/s_j$$

or

$$d_j = (\overline{X}_{2j} - \overline{X}_{1j})/s$$

depending on whether there is enough homogeneity of within-group variance from replication to replication to justify treating all of the s_js as equal. When different forms of measurement have been developed for each individual replication (as in the study conducted by Allen et al., 1990), it is obviously necessary to use separate values of s_j; when a common dependent measure has been employed, the pooled s should be preferred unless there is very good evidence against homogeneity. Both methods are shown for the hypothetical cell statistics arrayed in Table 6.1: $d_{[separate]}$ is the effect-size computed with a replication specific value of s_j, and $d_{[pooled]}$ is the effect-size computed with a common value of s generated as the square root of the within-groups variance.

However obtained, these effect-size measures can be averaged and their variance computed, as basic summaries of the information contained in the entire set of replications, as follows:

$$\overline{d} = \Sigma d_j/m \text{ and } \text{Var}(d) = \Sigma(d_j - \overline{d})^2/(m - 1)$$

Notice that the average effect-size is one way of measuring the overall main effect for treatment and that the effect-size variance is one way of measuring the treatment × message interaction. For the effect-sizes computed using the pooled standard deviation in Table 6.1, the average effect-size is .294 and the variance in the effect-sizes is .117.

The fact that we use meta-analysis statistics rather than analysis of variance does not change the basic objectives of the analysis, which are to determine what effect, if any, the treatment has, and to determine how uniform that effect is from message to message. Hence, we will want not only to compute the average treatment effect $\overline{d}$ and the variance in the treatment effect from replication to replication Var(d), but also to test these for significance, the first against the null hypothesis of a treatment effect of 0 and the second against the null hypothesis of complete uniformity of effect from replication to replication. It turns out that whether we pursue these objectives by way of meta-

TABLE 6.1. Illustrative Data for Comparison of Analysis of Variance and Meta-Analysis Procedures

Message	Group 1 Mean	Group 1 SS	Group 2 Mean	Group 2 SS	d_s	d_p
1	12.57	71.39	12.11	79.72	−.231	−.226
2	10.76	83.11	10.68	75.88	−.039	−.039
3	10.16	75.39	10.54	74.29	.196	.187
4	9.98	82.24	10.88	86.22	.439	.442
5	9.07	80.34	10.34	77.17	.624	.624
6	12.29	88.61	12.21	76.21	−.038	−.039
7	12.49	74.82	12.81	79.04	.159	.157
8	10.39	72.64	11.16	75.36	.390	.378
9	10.52	87.05	11.84	80.91	.628	.648
10	10.49	70.79	12.14	83.43	.840	.811

Note. n per cell = 20; d_s is the effect size computed using the replication-specific within-groups standard deviation; d_p is the effect size computed using the pooled within-groups standard deviation.

analysis or by way of analysis of variance, we will have to confront the same choices and—assuming we are consistent in our choices—we will come to the same conclusions. This point is developed fully in Jackson (1991), and will be explained only briefly below.

To establish some basic relationships between analysis of variance and meta-analysis, it will be helpful to see that the tests commonly employed in mixed-model analysis of variance can be expressed as simple functions of the effect-size measures and the study size.[5] The following relationships are exact if the pooled standard deviation is used, and approximate if the separate standard deviations are used:

$$F_{\text{treatment}} = MS_T/MS_{T \times M} = m \, \bar{d}^2/\text{Var}(d)$$
$$F_{\text{interaction}} = MS_{T \times M}/MS_{wg} = n \, \text{Var}(d)/2$$

Using the values of $\bar{d}$ and $\text{Var}(d)$ computed for the effect-size measures in the rightmost column of Table 6.1, we could test the main and interaction effects as follows:

$$F(1,9) = (10)(.294)^2/(.117) = 7.40$$
$$F(9,180) = (20)(.117)/2 = 1.17$$

These values are identical to a standard analysis of variance; compare them with the full analysis of variance as summarized in Table 6.2.

TABLE 6.2. Analysis of Variance on Table 6.1 Data

Source	Sum of squares	df	Mean squares	F
Treatment	35.880	1	35.880	7.398
Message	338.848	9	37.650	9.086
Treatment × Message	43.652	9	4.850	1.170
Within groups	1574.610	380	4.144	

Now, these are not the tests commonly employed in meta-analysis, and the question is sure to arise as to whether these are appropriate tests. Not surprisingly, the answer is that the appropriateness of these tests, or anything similar to them, depends on what is assumed about the relationship between the individual effect-size measures and the effect we wish to test. If we assume (as do meta-analysts practicing the methods of Hunter, Schmidt, & Jackson, 1982) that the underlying effect of interest can be represented as a single fixed value which differs—if at all—only through the operation of moderator variables, then the test of the interaction (modified to fit the differing study sizes and so on) would presumably be appropriate, but the test of the treatment would not. On the other hand, if we assume (as suggested by Hedges & Olkin, 1985, especially Chapter 9) that the underlying effect of interest may be variable around a central value, then tests of this general sort are fine. Notice that in trying to devise meta-analysis procedures to replace analysis of variance for replicated designs, we face precisely the same choice as between fixed-model and mixed-model assumptions in the analysis of variance: To say that the effect of interest is fixed is to say that the estimate of the treatment effect does not depend on the sample of messages included in the analysis, and to say that the effect of interest is variable is to say that the estimate of the treatment effect does depend on the messages included.

Among meta-analysis procedures currently available, the methods best tailored to the analysis of replicated experiments would seem to be those proposed by Hedges and Olkin (1985) as "random effects meta-analysis." Hedges and Olkin propose an approximate χ^2 test for homogeneity of effect-size variance and a method for constructing a confidence interval around the average treatment effect, both of which are constructed on the explicit assumption that the variability of the treatment effect from replication to replication is a source of error in the estimation of the treatment effect itself. Although the Hedges and Olkin procedures do not give the same results as the analysis of variance procedures, they represent a reasonable and conceptually congruent alternative to the mixed-model analysis of variance.[6]

Two important points can be taken from the foregoing discussion. First, it is certainly possible to find or devise meta-analysis methods to use as primary analytic tools within replicated experiments. Doing so buys the researcher a certain amount of flexibility, and there is little question that development of appropriately tailored meta-analysis methods would be quite useful for replicated treatment comparison experiments. But second, and more important, using meta-analysis statistics does not allow the analyst to sidestep the issue of whether to treat message replications as fixed or as random: This choice must be confronted within meta-analysis as well before a test of the treatment main effects can be constructed. Given the evident parallelism of purpose and of materials between the two sets of procedures, it is to be expected that a meta-analysis constructed on the same conceptual choices that lead to the mixed-model analysis of variance will differ from the analysis of variance only in details. In other words, it does not seem at all reasonable to suppose that meta-analysis will offer any escape from the problems addressed in Chapter 5.

CASE STUDIES AND "SIMPLE EFFECTS" ANALYSIS

In an experiment with relatively few replications, one way to argue a general conclusion about the treatment is to show that the main effect of the treatment is consistent (at the level of precision claimed) for each of the individual replications (see Hewes, 1983). For example, a treatment applied to three different kernel messages might have the same basic pattern of effect, but in differing degree. This might be shown, quantitatively or qualitatively, by displaying the "simple main effects" of the treatment for each of the three message replications. One might reasonably conclude, from a few very consistent replications, that a certain sort of manipulation of the message leads to increases (or decreases) in effectiveness (or other outcome).

The plausibility of such a conclusion depends on many context-dependent factors: the number of cases observed, the uniformity of the effect across the individual cases, the adequacy of the cases as representatives of the domain of messages to which we might want to apply the treatment, and the nature of the treatment itself. The more variable the effect of a treatment from message to message, the more cases will have to be considered in order to get a reliable estimate of the average treatment effect, and the more cases will have to be considered in order to discover moderators of the treatment effect. We might expect that convention-based features of language use (e.g., the use of verbal "immediacy"—a set of conventional means for expressing positive affect) will have more regular effects across messages than will substantive content variations (e.g., the use of altruism or self-interest as the fundamental appeal) or aesthetic/stylistic variations (e.g., the use of humor). Evidence of uniformity within small samples should carry greater weight when we have independent reasons (such as conventionality of the feature) for expecting it than when we have independent reasons for suspecting diversity.

An increasing number of experiments in communication include message replications, though the number of replications is generally quite small. One analytic strategy, superficially similar to what I have been describing, would be to base the evaluation of uniformity on an explicit test of the treatment × message interaction. Certain commonplace ideas in social science research might suggest a strategy of testing and interpreting treatment effects only in the absence of a significant treatment × message interaction, and presumably, the main reason one would want to do this is to justify the apparently more powerful fixed-model (Option B) analysis of the treatment effect. This is not a satisfactory approach.

One reason this approach is not satisfactory is that a nonsignificant treatment × message interaction is no good basis for assuming uniformity of effect, for all of the familiar reasons associated with accepting the null hypothesis. Consider the hypothetical data set in Table 6.3. The data have been constructed to represent a replicated treatment comparison using five kernel messages. The treatment variable has two levels, and, as can be seen from the table of cell means, the effect

TABLE 6.3. Exemplary Data with Nonsignificant Treatment × Message Interaction

Message	Treatment 1[a]	Treatment 2[a]
1	10.1	12.2
2	10.2	9.9
3	9.2	9.0
4	10.4	11.8
5	10.3	11.4

Analysis of variance

Source	SS	df	MS	F(b)	F(c)
Treatment	33.62	1	33.62	7.03	3.09
Interaction	43.48	4	10.87	2.27	2.27
Within group	908.00	190	4.78		

[a] n per cell = 20

of the treatment changes from message to message. However, the treatment × message interaction is not significant, so it is tempting to simply say that "message" makes no difference to the treatment effect and to test it treating messages as "fixed" (or even ignoring them altogether if the main effect for messages is also nonsignificant). If we were to follow such a strategy with these data, we would conclude that Treatment 2 is significantly better than Treatment 1, even though Treatment 2 appears as better for only three of the five messages. (The Option C test of the treatment effect—treating replications as a random factor—gives a different result, and this result is a much better fit with the evident quality of the data.)

A nonsignificant interaction does not justify the conclusion that the treatment is uniform across messages. Consider the intrinsic weakness of these data as a basis for predicting what would happen with a hypothetical Message 6. Nonuniformity that is in practice quite unimportant may nevertheless be sufficient to account for the apparent effect of a treatment, especially in a small message sample.

But what about significant treatment × message interactions? Does the presence of a significant treatment × message interaction defeat efforts to interpret the main effect of treatment? No. A nonsignificant interaction does not establish uniformity of effect, and although a significant interaction establishes nonuniformity, this nonuniformity may or may not threaten the kind of conclusion we wish to draw. A significant interaction may certainly come about as a consequence of varying effect magnitude, without any inconsistency at all at the level of precision we are interested in, that is, just as we may get a nonsignificant interaction despite meaningful nonuniformity of effect, we may also get a significant interaction despite practical uniformity. A nonsignificant interaction is no requirement for a plausible interpretation of a main effect for treatment.

Consider the hypothetical data set in Table 6.4. Within the five replications considered, the experimental manipulation produces a consistent advantage for Treatment 2 over Treatment 1, but the size of this advantage is quite variable. The significant F ratio for the interaction effect should not discourage us from noticing that while the size of the treatment effect is inconsistent, the general direction of effect is not. (Note that in this particular case, the Option C F ratio for the main effect of treatment is also significant, despite the small number of replications and the significant variability from replication to replication.)

The comparison between the two hypothetical data sets is instructive. For the first, the interaction was nonsignificant, yet there

TABLE 6.4. Exemplary Data with Significant Treatment × Message Interaction

Message	Treatment 1[a]	Treatment 2[a]
1	10.1	11.2
2	10.9	12.8
3	11.5	14.9
4	9.2	10.1
5	11.7	12.2

Analysis of variance

Source	SS	df	MS	F(b)	F(c)
Treatment	121.68	1	121.68	25.46	9.23
Interaction	52.72	4	13.18	2.75	2.75
Within group	908.00	190	4.78		

[a] n per cell = 20

was no consistent effect associated with the treatment from message to message. For the second, the interaction was significant, yet despite this a consistent advantage for Treatment 2 appeared across all five of the message replications. It should be clear that the interpretability of the main effect for treatment does not depend on the presence or absence of a treatment × message interaction. In the Option C analysis, the nonuniformity of the treatment from message to message is treated as a source of error in the estimation of the treatment effect, whether it happens to be significant or not. This is precisely how treatment × respondent interactions are used in conventional repeated-measures designs; only very rarely are treatment × respondent interactions tested at all.

What if the cases lack any sort of uniformity in their responsiveness to the treatment, as in the first example data set above? In situations of this sort, it is simply not reasonable to put forward any generalization about the treatment effect—not even the quasi claim that there is no general effect. Suppose we contrast two persuasive strategies, using three concrete messages as the bases for the contrasts. If we find that the Strategy A version is better for kernel messages 1 and 2 but that the Strategy B version is better for kernel message 3, we are in a very poor position as far as interpretation goes. We cannot very well conclude that Strategy A is better in general: If each strategy is better in half the cases, a sample of three cases is quite likely to be divided in such a way as to show one strategy better in two cases and the other in one case. Neither can we conclude that the effects of the treatment are unpredictable, since Message 3 may simply be an exception to a general rule giving the advantage to Strategy A, or, possibly, the implementations of the strategic contrast for Message 3 may have been faulty in some idiosyncratic way. In a case of this kind, the data do defeat the effort at generalization; nothing at all can be made of the experiment.

One implication to take from this discussion is that while it is sometimes possible to argue a good case from a very small number of message replications, it is unwise to bank on being able to do so. Efforts to argue the case in an openly inductive fashion are constrained by the level of message-to-message uniformity. Case-study logic depends on there being a great deal of case-to-case uniformity, and some substantive basis for believing this to be representative. Efforts to argue the case using Option C statistics will be constrained by the low power resulting from the small number of replications. Efforts to argue the case using Option B statistics supported by explicit testing of the treatment × message interaction are obstructed by the lack of fit between the substantive claims being made and the statistical evidence offered in their support. Clearly, an experiment incorporating three or four replications is better than an experiment incorporating only one, but still such experiments offer very insecure grounds for generic claims about messages.

"BOOTSTRAP" STATISTICS AND RANDOMIZATION TESTS

A final class of analytic alternatives to be considered are the so-called bootstrap methods (Efron, 1982) and randomization tests (Edgington, 1980). Bootstrap statistics are distribution-free statistics, which means they make no assumptions about the shape of the distribution from which a set of observations have been drawn. Randomization tests are methods for computing statistical significance without assuming either any particular population distribution or any sort of random sampling. Efron describes his procedures as substituting "brute computational force" for theoretical assumptions, and Edgington describes his as offering alternative statistics for experiments in which the observational units cannot be or have not been selected at random. For our purposes, the possible importance of these methods should be quite clear. In dealing with "message populations," we are positioned very poorly to defend assumptions we might like to make about the underlying distribution of values within the population, and the situation is worsened by the fact that in sampling nonrandomly we may implicitly define a population with a distribution different from the underlying distribution. It is not clear that these circumstances preclude the use of familiar statistics (as I have tried to argue in Chapter 5), but certainly they invite special consideration of approaches that do not depend on assumptions of these kinds.

Both bootstrap methods and randomization tests rely on empirical "resamplings" of data rather than on heavy assumptive frameworks associated with conventional statistical tests. The sampling distribution of a statistic (such as a mean, a correlation, or an effect-size) is built inductively from the observed cases, rather than deductively from a prior theoretical model of the population. In some cases, this leads to tests and measures not unlike the corresponding parametric statistics.

Randomization tests are based on "data permutation," meaning that numbers that are interchangeable under the null-hypothesis are repeatedly re-shuffled to generate a null hypothesis distribution of outcomes, and the probability of getting a result as great as the one actually obtained is computed empirically. For example, in an experiment with two groups of respondents randomly formed from a common pool, the actual mean difference observed in the experiment would be compared with all possible divisions of the pool, or with a random subset of all possible divisions. Randomization tests for mixed-model analysis-of-variance situations have not, to my knowledge, been previously developed; we will consider possible implementations of a randomization test for replicated experiments shortly.

Bootstrap procedures are based not on permutation but on resampling with replacement. Given a sample of n observations, one bootstrap sample would consist of n observations chosen one at a time from the original n. This means that if we have cases A, B, and C, the possible bootstrap samples are AAA, AAB, AAC, ABB, ABC, and so on. The sample is taken as given, and samples *of the same size* are drawn from it, with replacement, over and over, each of the bootstrap samples generating a value for the statistic of interest. These values form a distribution of outcomes for the statistic, and the value actually obtained in the original sample can be compared with this distribution in the same way that one might compare the value of a conventional test statistic with a theoretical distribution of outcomes under the null hypothesis. Note the close fit between bootstrap procedures and the conceptualization of the sample/population relationship advanced in Chapter 5. Bootstrap methods too have yet to be developed for the sort of problem we confront, but there does not appear to be any theoretical obstacle to such an extension.

For both randomization tests and bootstrap procedures, two main issues must be addressed. The first issue is what statistics to compute on the observations and on the permuted or resampled data. It is perfectly possible to compute familiar test statistics, such as t or F ratios, altering only the manner in which null-hypothesis probabilities are generated for these results. But it is also possible to substitute simpler (but interchangeable) descriptive statistics such as mean differences, average effect-sizes, effect-size variances, and so on (see Edgington, 1980). In considering possible implementations of these methods for replicated experiments, we will want to operate with the simplest possible statistics that are relevant to our research questions.

The second issue is whether permutations and resamplings should be based on replications as units or on respondents. In most applications developed so far, respondents have counted as individual observational units. Most previously developed randomization tests have permuted respondents, and most previously developed bootstrap procedures have resampled respondents. The inclusion of messages as a second replication factor will result in a need for special tests responsive to the special hypotheses to be tested. In many cases, it will be messages—not respondents—or both message replications and respondents that will need to be permuted or resampled in order to test the null hypothesis of interest. Conceivably, a single experiment will require permutations or resamplings based on messages to test one hypothesis and permutations or resamplings based on persons to test another hypothesis.

SUMMARY

We have considered three alternatives to conducting mixed-model analysis of variance on replicated experiments: (1) application of meta-analysis procedures *within* experiments treating each replication as an independent basis for estimating a treatment effect; (2) case-by-case analysis of an effect for each of a very small number of replications; and (3) development of "distribution-free" procedures similar to randomization tests or bootstrap-like procedures. The fundamental motivations for seeking alternatives are to avoid the "foundationalist critique" of treating messages as random and to improve the power of our test procedures with small samples of messages.

Meta-analysis statistics are (or could be) functional substitutes for analysis-of-variance statistics. They offer no relief from the foundationalist critique, and they offer no increase in power to detect effects, but they do offer certain intuitively appealing ways of *describing* results. Expressing experimental outcomes in terms of an average effect-size and an effect-size variance is an especially clear way of presenting results of replicated treatment comparisons, although these descriptive tools are not, of course, unique to meta-analysis.

Case-by-case analysis using very small numbers of messages can, in some circumstances, lead to a plausible argument for a consistent effect; however, the strength of the argument remains a function of the size of the sample, the degree of consistency, and the independent reasons for believing the sample to be an adequate representation of the domain of interest. In general, it will be preferable to tackle the small-sample problem by increasing the number of replications.

Randomization tests and bootstrap procedures are reasonable (if presently underdeveloped) alternatives to analysis of variance, and bootstrap procedures in particular offer a close fit with the perspective on inference developed in Chapter 5. Although it is not yet clear exactly what tests of these sorts might look like, they have the possibly important advantage of requiring no assumptions about message populations. They are not, at present, readily available, but there is no obvious barrier to their development. These procedures can also be used to build a more general case for or against the use of familiar analysis-of-variance procedures.

The more general lesson to be taken from this chapter is that objections to treating messages as random are not arguments for treating them as fixed. If it should prove impossible to develop a defense of treating messages as random within an analysis of variance, the fallback is to some new statistical procedure specially designed for the circumstances.

SEVEN

Message Classes and the Problem of Representation

In this chapter we will explore the idea of a message class from which concrete messages are to be sampled, and about which some sort of inference is to be made. As in other forms of experimental research in the social sciences, experimental research on messages involves two sorts of inferences. The first sort of inference takes the form of an abstract description of a set of concrete observations: From the observation that a certain ten specific messages are, on the average, more persuasive than ten alternative messages, we conclude that the strategy they represent is more effective than the strategy represented by the others. The means by which this first sort of inference is justified have been discussed in earlier chapters. The second sort of inference is what would commonly be referred to as "generalization": an expectation about the properties of a broad class of events based on observation of a small set of such events. This chapter is concerned with generalization, that is, with features of the research process that limit the scope of a conclusion.

The discussion will begin with a brief analysis of the concept of a message class, as a starting point for an analysis of the task of generalizing about messages. We will consider a number of obstacles to be overcome in generalizing and some concrete strategies that address these obstacles.

MESSAGES CLASSES ARE NOT POPULATIONS

Implicit in any research question about a message variable is some domain within which the question can meaningfully be answered. This domain may be a very broad class of messages defined by commonality of function, such as persuasive messages. Or it might be a more restricted but still indefinitely large category, such as promises or threats. We might be tempted to refer to these domains as "populations" in order to emphasize that individual concrete messages incorporated in experiments are samples from a broader class of possible materials. But the term is not really apt when applied to message categories, because it connotes both concreteness and finite membership: We generally think of populations as finite collections of concrete cases, available for identification and enumeration. And message categories are not usually finite collections of concrete cases, but open-ended sets defined by some abstract feature whose concrete forms are innumerable.

These features of message classes obviously constrain our strategies for "sampling" messages. We cannot sample at random from message classes, because the members of the class do not exist until we create them, and we have no way of managing things so that all conceivable messages have an equal chance of being created. However, if our objective is to develop some general claim about an abstract class of messages, issues of representativeness and unbiasedness must be addressed.

Let us begin by considering the limits on the class to be represented by the sample. Ideally, the sample should be representative of the entire domain of messages for which the research question is meaningful. Rather obviously, the nature of the variables explored will partially define the domain of interest, since some strategy variables are relevant only within some limited class of messages. For example, the class implied by questions about the advantages of two-sidedness within persuasive messages is not the class of all persuasive messages. Argument sidedness as a strategic dimension of the message has no clear meaning unless certain basic conditions are met: The message must, for example, be verbal, and it must be explicitly argumentative. Different strategic dimensions imply different classes, which is just to say that a message variable may or may not have definable values for every conceivable message that could be constructed. A concept of domain is inherent in any particular research question, whether made explicit by the researcher or not.

Now, the class of interest implied by any research question may or may not be clearly bounded, and this fact will create additional difficulties for the researcher. Some strategic variables will have a clear and definite meaning within some core set of messages, but looser applicability within some fuzzily bounded periphery. For example, the set of messages for which one-sided and two-sided argumentation represent realistic strategic possibilities may have as its core the explicitly argumentative verbal messages described above, but sidedness as a dimension of difference between message and message will have applicability beyond the core. For argument sidedness, the fringe cases might include such objects as commercial advertisements, within which a choice must be made about whether to offer explicit comparisons with competing products. For persuasive messages generally, fringe cases might be found among messages that have persuasive intent without paradigmatic persuasive form: films and paintings, for example.

It is by no means plain that there is any great virtue in sampling the entire domain to which a research question might apply, if what is really of interest is the operation of a variable within some core set of messages, say, some class of messages for which the choice of one strategy or another is a recurrent fundamental problem. On the other hand, it should be plain that a generalization to the entire domain based on a sample taken entirely from the core would be quite unwarranted. A sample chosen for the ease with which the treatment might be applied is not a good basis for generalization to a broader domain within which the treatment becomes increasingly problematic.

Given the complexities of defining the appropriate class and the impossibility of sampling randomly from it, it seems unlikely that there can be any routine solution to the problem of how to sample message classes. On the other hand, it is clear enough that there are better and worse bases for generalization, better and worse ways of evaluating strategic options. Our problem is to try to articulate a rationale for generalizations about messages based on samples whose relationships to the classes of interest are unspecifiable. The common lore concerning sampling methods offers little help in this task, not only because the concrete procedures involved in random sampling methods fail to fit the features of our materials (message classes), but also because the corresponding logic of inference fails to fit the features of our generalization problem. Some alternative ways of thinking about the relationship between sample and population must be devised, and also, perhaps, some alternative ways of thinking about "justification."

Jacobs and I (1983) suggested, regarding the problem of justifying generalization, a more straightforwardly inductive approach to the subject matter. We advocated a fundamental shift away from thinking of the sample as selected from a predefined population and toward thinking of the population as defined by the nature of the messages included in the sample. Features of messages that lead to choosing them or excluding them help to define the class of messages to which some generalization is expected to apply. If in research on argument sidedness we restrict our samples to verbal messages that make explicit arguments in favor of explicitly stated claims, we have not biased the sample in any meaningful sense, for it is within messages of just that sort that the choice of one-sidedness or two-sidedness would be available. Conclusions about sidedness drawn from samples of messages restricted in this way are not expected to apply to nonverbal messages or to messages that attempt to persuade through nonargumentative means, but this limitation is inherent in the nature of the variable, not in any sort of mismatch between sample and population.

This line of reasoning, fairly innocuous so far, can be extended in some useful directions. We have considered a restriction on the sampled materials that follows from the researcher's expectations about the domain to which conclusions are to apply. What about restrictions on the sampled materials that follow from deliberate or accidental preference for certain sorts of messages? Research procedures often —in fact, probably always—involve unexamined restrictions on the sorts of messages sampled. For example, an experiment may maintain an approximate equivalence in length from one message replication to another, so that all of the sampled materials are messages of 1000 to 1500 words. Or an experiment may involve a single arbitrarily chosen presentation mode (written, spoken), so that all of the sampled materials come from an identifiable subset of the domain of interest. Or the method of generating messages may involve some unexamined restriction: All of the messages may have been chosen from published editorials, or all of the messages may have been written by college sophomores. As regards generalization to all persuasive messages, or even to all verbal messages involving explicit argumentation, these unexamined restrictions on the sampled materials would seem to raise obstacles.

The stance we take toward these unexamined restrictions on the sample will be crucial to communication research methodology. If we think of the message class as a predefined category with a describable membership, we will surely think of these restrictions as "barriers" to generalization from sample to population (as does Morley, 1988). But we need not think about samples and populations in just this way. Instead of thinking of the composed sample as having been drawn from a predefined population, we might think of the messages within the sample as a set of exemplars from which a class of "similar" messages can be imaginatively constructed. This imaginatively constructed class includes as members any individual message that would be an acceptable substitute for the individual messages of the sample as composed, and such a class has usefulness for us, methodologically, even if we never assign it a name or specify all of the conditions on its membership. Its usefulness is as a step in an argument, a tool to be used in justifying a general claim about a message variable based on a certain finite number of observations.

Let us say that we have documented an effect within a set of concrete messages: for example, a persuasive advantage for two-sidedness over one-sidedness in a set of 20 experimental messages. How far can we "generalize" the conclusion? The answer suggested so far is that we can generalize to the entire class of "similar" messages that could have substituted for the messages in our experiment—not, of course, to each individual message considered individually, but to the class. If this seems not quite satisfactory—the generalization being either too restricted to be of interest or too indefinite in scope—we must then think about adding steps to the argument. Specifically, we can proceed in at least three ways to extend the grounds for the general claim.

First, we can broaden the sample itself so that the class projected by it comes closer and closer to the intended scope of the claim. This accords with the common-sense expectation that the larger and more diverse the message set observed, the better the basis for generalization. Second, we can replicate the procedure within several quite different (but likewise restricted) samples, using each of these restricted generalizations to build a presumption of generality across imagined "subpopulations." Third, we can partition the sample as composed in various ways, so as to test the sensitivity of the generalization to variations in form and content of experimental messages; again, the objective is to create a presumption of generality by showing that the treatment effect is not specific to any sort of subgroup or partition. None of these strategies depends upon the imaginatively constructed message classes having any particular substantive identity; these hypothetical classes function quite well as abstractions, which is to say that we can say something meaningful about the operation of a variable within its taken-for-granted domain, even when we cannot articulate clear criteria for membership within that domain.

What I have outlined here is an argumentative strategy, and its scientific value is obviously not as a procedural guarantee of correct generalizations from sample to class, but as an explication of premises that would allow meaningful generalization about messages. The general point of view advocated here echoes many other analyses of induction and the role of statistical inference within induction. This role is more limited than is commonly acknowledged within the social sciences; logicians and statisticians alike recognize that statistical inference does not substitute for induction. For example, Hacking (1965) notes a distinction between "open" and "closed" populations and argues that inferences about the characteristics of open populations always involve some nonstatistical premises in addition to anything that might be justified by the sampling method. In generalizing from a non-random sample of cases, there can be a statistical inference from sample to "sampling frame," but the further generalization to the class of interest is not statistical but inductive. Cornfield and Tukey (1956) likewise note that inference from a sample is a two-step process (metaphorically, a "two-span bridge"), with the first step relying on statistical inference to a limited class and the second step relying on substantive grounds for believing the conclusion to be generalizable beyond the limited class. The argumentative moves I advocate involve incorporation of one or more extra premises into a defense of a general claim, premises useful not only in extending the scope of a generalization (as in Hacking's analysis of induction), but also in undergirding the first span of Cornfield and Tukey's "two-span bridge" between observation and generalization.

ADDRESSING OBSTACLES TO GENERALIZATION FROM CONVENIENCE SAMPLES

Most message samples used in experiments will be best regarded as convenience samples, in more or less the same sense of that term as applied to human respondents. In some cases, it will be possible to sample at random from a concrete collection of messages (such as the University of Oklahoma's Kanter Political Commercial Archive or the news reports indexed in the *TV News Index and Abstracts*), but the prototypical questions posed about message effects are intended to apply to abstract message classes that cannot be approached this way. Convenience samples do not function in the same way that random samples do; we cannot argue from them as though they were random samples. However, with careful consideration of the burden of proof involved in a general claim about messages, it should be possible to develop convenience samples in such a way as to permit a reasonable defense of such a claim.

A reasonable starting point for attacking any methodological problem is analysis of the problem itself. In this case, the problem is justification of a generalization from a set of cases whose representativeness is not underwritten by random selection. We might profitably begin by considering the sorts of things that can go wrong in generalizing from convenience samples, in order to form a clear picture of dangers to be avoided.

In this section, I will point out several things that can go wrong and propose some general forms of solution. I do not claim that either the list of obstacles or the means offered to address them are complete; other obstacles will surely emerge from empirical work using message samples, and researchers will find many alternative ways to overcome these obstacles. I will, however, take particular care to respond to sampling-related issues that have been mentioned as objections to the use of replicated experiments.

Bias

One serious threat to generalization from convenience samples is bias on the part of the experimenter. By bias, I mean a choice of messages that is partial to a hypothesis. This threat was discussed in some detail by Morley (1988), who pointed out that large numbers of experimental messages written by a single experimenter were likely to reflect the experimenter's "message-generating biases." Although problems of this sort are not uniquely associated with multiple-message designs, they must certainly be taken seriously in research aimed at drawing generic conclusions about message categories or effects of treatments on messages within a category. Consider some concrete cases in which vulnerability to bias might seriously threaten conclusions drawn from a sample of messages.

Suppose an experimenter wishes to evaluate the relative effectiveness of threats and promises as persuasive strategies. To answer this question experimentally, the researcher will need to observe responses to a large sample of threats and a large sample of promises. Where do the individual threats and promises come from? If the experimenter writes all of the experimental messages, there is a very good possibility that expectations about the outcome of the experiment will affect the quality of the examples written. The research question itself implies some prior expectation that threats and promises will differ from one another, and it is certainly plausible to worry that a researcher who expects promises to be better than threats will manage to write "good" promises and "bad" threats, even if, in principle, both appeal types have equal potential.

Nor is this problem unique to messages *written* by the experimenter: In threats and promises collected from naturally occurring discourse, the selection of the examples to be used may equally reflect the experimenter's biases. For example, threats that look potentially effective might be excluded as being "atypical" or might be re-labeled as something other than threats. As long as the experimenter is personally responsible for the development of the sample, the materials are vulnerable to the biasing effects of the experimenter's expectations.

Nor is this problem limited to cases in which the messages are sampled within categories. It can occur equally in designs involving manipulation of a message variable. An experimenter's expectations can obviously affect the choice of kernel messages: the individual messages may be chosen precisely because they lend themselves well to one strategic variation or another. Suppose the experimenter wishes to show that language intensity increases the persuasive impact of a message. Bias may appear because the experimenter chooses only message topics for which a certain amount of emotional expression is expected. But bias can also occur in the implementation of the treatment variable, just as in the threat–promise comparison, because it will always be possible that the experimenter's expectations lead to composition of good examples of one treatment and bad examples of the other.

Experimenter expectations are unavoidable, and they have been shown to have consequences for many phases of the research process (Rosenthal, 1976). But many procedural safeguards against these expectations have been devised to prevent them from influencing outcomes. For example, double-blind experiments, in which both experimenter and subject are blind to the subject's assignment to a treatment group, are specifically tailored to protect the subject's response to the treatment from the biasing effects of expectations.

What procedures might be devised to limit bias in the message sample due to experimenter expectations? One way is to distance the experimenter from the concrete message sample. A researcher might collect base messages in a way certain to be unaffected by personal bias (say, by using all essays printed in a volume of *Editorials on File* within a given time interval), and implement the treatment in an impersonal way by having individuals naive to the study's purpose edit the messages for consistency with a categorical definition. Messages could be discarded if it were shown that they fit no category of interest, or if they proved to be impossible to edit to fit the treatment. (Note that the process of justifying any decision to discard a message could itself aid in refinement of concepts.) Or the experimenter could have messages made to order "from scratch" by naive respondents and later categorized for purposes of the experiment by additional naive coders. Each of these options will be discussed in more detail later in this chapter.

A good illustration of how a message sample can be protected from experimenter expectations appeared in a study by B. O'Keefe and McCornack (1987). O'Keefe and McCornack hypothesized that "regulatory messages" exhibiting different "message design logics" would lead to different evaluations of the message and the speaker. Message design logics, according to their theory, are very fundamental understandings of how communication works. These understandings give rise to principles of communication design that are manifest in messages produced under certain kinds of conditions. Each message design logic has a distinctive premise associated with it, termed a "communication-constituting premise": the expressive design logic is characterized by a presumption that communication is for the direct expression of thought, the conventional design logic by a reliance on rules for appropriate communicative performance, and the rhetorical design logic by a presumption that communication functions to create situation and relationship. The theory suggests that in communication situations involving certain sorts of complexities, the messages generated by each of the three logics will differ in effectiveness, with the rhetorical logic offering the best prospects and expressive logic the worst.

In empirically testing the relative effectiveness of messages representing each design logic, one approach might have been for O'Keefe and McCornack to write examples of messages typical of each design logic and submit them to respondents for evaluation. But this would open the experiment to charges of bias, for the experimenters' expectations about the relative effectiveness of the three message types might lead them to write effective messages of one type and ineffective messages of the other types, when, in principle, effective messages of all types might be possible. So O'Keefe and McCornack simply presented a large group of respondents with a hypothetical situation and asked them to generate messages in response. These messages, varying naturally in the three design logics, were categorized by one of the experimenters, and since this step too can be vulnerable to bias, the coding of the messages was checked by use of an independent coder unconnected with the study. These messages, just as written by the respondents, were submitted to a new pool of respondents for evaluation, effectively neutralizing the potential biases associated with the experimenters' expectations.

What makes experimenter bias so insidious in social scientific research is its invisibility: If we were aware of our own biases—their sources and their forms of subtle expression—we would be able to guard against them. But although we cannot avoid having expectations or prevent our expectations from affecting our behavior, we can protect our experimental outcomes from effects of bias by adopting procedural safeguards of the sort illustrated by the O'Keefe and McCornack study. The trick is to use messages generated independently of the preferences and intuitions of the experimenter.

Collection-Category Mismatch

A second general threat to generalizations based on message samples is the use of message cases that project a class different from the one intended. I term this problem a *collection–category mismatch* because the sample as a collection of concrete cases may or may not fit the categorical description applied to it. This sort of mismatch can come in at least three forms. The collection may be so homogeneous as to define a subcategory within the category of interest; or the collection may fail to respect distinctions between the category of interest and other conceptually related categories; or the collection may simply fall outside the category to which generalization is intended. I have in mind here the same sort of problem as occurs when a treatment (say, an instructional method or a medication) is tested on a human population different from the one for which it was designed.

Now, to be clear from the outset, I wish to emphasize that an apparent mismatch between collection and category is not always a serious threat to a generalization from sample to class. In principle, any message feature that remains invariant within the sample might be thought to define a subcategory within the category of interest and hence to threaten the validity of conclusions drawn about the category. But to say that the conclusion is threatened, in principle, is not to say that the threat has any actual plausibility. That depends upon the circumstances. In practice, some subcategorizations can be assumed to be inconsequential while others can be expected to have important consequences for experimental outcomes. If the effects of language intensity on speaker credibility are evaluated only in speeches of 1000–1500 words (and not in speeches shorter than 1000 or longer than 1500 words), we probably will not assume that a broader sample would reverse the conclusions. But if the message sample is restricted not only by length but say, by topic, with only emotionally charged topics included, we might well reserve judgment on the general effect of language intensity, regardless of what conclusion can be drawn about the effect of intensity within the subcategory of messages projected by the emotionally charged sample.

Notice, too, that the way we label this particular problem depends upon our point of view. We might consider it a problem of inappropriate sampling, and probably *should* consider it a problem of sampling if the intended scope of the generalization was set beforehand. If, for example, our interest was in documenting the effects of message sidedness on students' comprehension of lecture material, experimenting on sidedness within persuasive essays could hardly be considered appropriate. But the problem can be turned around and seen instead as an over-generalization: a conclusion justified over a certain domain being extended to some other domain. And again, whether such an extension represents a good or bad generalization depends upon substantive considerations as much as logical or methodological considerations.

Developing a sample that offers a convincing match with the category of interest can never be a matter of routine. However, several useful guidelines can be proposed. First, the researcher should begin the sampling process with a clear conceptualization of the category of interest and with some clear ideas about the diversity of form and content to be found within the category. If the category of interest is "initial interactions between strangers," one might expect the conceptualized class to encompass interactions differentiated on many dimensions: on whether the interaction has a business or social purpose, on whether the interaction is a first meeting or only meeting, and so on.

Second, to avoid a sample that falls within a narrow subcategory from the category of interest, the messages might be chosen so as to vary as many irrelevant features as possible. Persuasive messages might be assembled from a wide range of published and unpublished sources representing the natural settings for influence: editorials and letters from newspapers, speeches delivered at public meetings, direct mail appeals for donations, and so on. Initial interactions might be collected opportunistically from nonlaboratory settings such as new-employee get-togethers, public waiting rooms, or college dormitories. Notice how a strategy of this sort cooperates with strategies for avoiding bias, discussed above.

Third, to build a presumption of generality across subcategory lines, the researcher might consider several separate samples, each rather homogeneous but in different ways. For example, if the experimenter wishes to vary some strategic dimension of persuasive messages, the need for standardized dependent measures or for standardized presentation media might require invariance on certain features. Simple replication of the experiment with several different convenience samples of messages, each sample composed differently, can build a presumption of generality across messages in just the same way that this strategy functions to build a presumption of generality across human subgroups.

Quite obviously, these strategies do not guarantee a representative sample of the class of interest, nor do they attempt to. Instead, they offer means by which specific threats to a conclusion can be avoided or by which such threats can be disarmed. To emphasize this, let us consider one final strategy, and it is not a sampling strategy at all, but a generalization strategy: Qualify the conclusion in terms of its known limitations.

When evidence for an effect is available only within a limited subclass of messages, the generalization should be made explicitly in two steps, the first being a (relatively) definite but limited generalization from case to category and the second being a more tentative but less restricted generalization from category to category. The first step depends upon the results of the experiment—the number of cases considered and the uniformity of the results from case to case. The second step depends upon a (nonempirical) presumption that there is nothing special about the category of messages observed that would uniquely foster the process or effect of interest. The second step will never be "justified" in any absolute sense, but the step—properly acknowledged and qualified—is nevertheless quite defensible when there is no basis for suspecting peculiarity in the category observed. Recall Hacking's two forms of inference or Cornfield and Tukey's two-span bridge.

Notice that our discussion of generalization centers on possible objections to a claim and strategies for answering these objections. This contrasts sharply with what I have elsewhere termed "foundationalist" approaches: approaches that accept as justified only claims whose truth can be guaranteed in terms of premises that have already been logically or empirically secured. Foundationalist approaches envision ideal circumstances and seek methods that would guarantee knowledge under such conditions: for example, an urn composed of red and green balls, the proportions of which would be estimated through sampling. The approach represented in this book takes for granted that we will want to make claims about certain kinds of things, whether or not these things resemble urns full of balls, and whether or not claims about them can be justified in a foundationalist sense. My assumption is that we will accept or reject empirical claims depending upon how they fare in comparison with rival views, and that the steps we take in research to build a strong case in support of a conclusion are directed by the counter-arguments that might plausibly be raised against it. This means that empirical arguments may sometimes exploit presumptions (such as the presumption that there is nothing unusual about a sample of messages that would make them respond peculiarly to a treatment) and other times incorporate counterfactual premises (such as the assumed existence of a class of messages "similar" to those included in the sample), for these presumptions and premises may define the conditions necessary for any comparison of a claim with its rivals.

The remainder of the chapter considers practical strategies for generating message samples. Diverse strategies are described, and no particular concrete procedure is advocated. On the contrary, it is assumed that different research situations will require different specific procedures, even given a constant attentiveness to issues such as bias and collection/category mismatch. The strategies described here should suffice to establish that there *are* practical means for generating multiple-message samples, by illustrating the means that have so far been devised.

STRATEGIES FOR GENERATING MESSAGE SAMPLES

An experimenter has two basic options in generating a message sample: collecting messages produced in natural communication contexts, or creating new messages especially for the purpose of the experiment. Both options can produce good bases for generalization if exercised with intelligence and good sense. The primary advantage of creating messages from scratch is that the experimenter can control certain features that may be important to the administration of the experiment (e.g., message length or medium) or to the form of dependent measure (e.g., some specific response called for in the message itself such as charitable giving). The primary disadvantage of messages constructed specially for the experiment is the risk of bias. The advantages and disadvantages of collected messages are complementary: Messages collected from natural communication contexts are more likely to be representative of the domain of interest, but also more likely to throw up difficulties for the conduct of the experiment.

I will divide my suggestions for generating message samples into three parts, the first dealing with collection of messages from published sources, the second with collection of messages from natural contexts of occurrence, and the third with construction or elicitation of messages within a "laboratory" frame. Nothing in what follows should be construed as advocacy of one method over another; all of these are, in my opinion, reasonable ways to proceed.

Published Messages and Collections of Messages

Messages suitable for use in persuasion experiments are readily available in any good reference library. For example, collections of persuasive and argumentative essays occur annually in *Editorials on File*—reprints of editorials from newspapers and other publications throughout the United States. *Vital Speeches* collects important addresses delivered on diverse occasions and dealing with a wide range of topics of public interest. Individual messages can obviously be found in commentary sections of news magazines, on editorial pages of newspapers, and, of course, in advertisements. Experiments on persuasive message variables can use these published messages (in their entirety or as abstracts) either as cases sampled to represent categories or as the kernel messages to which treatments are applied.

Among published sources of messages, special mention should be made of comprehensive archival collections. *Television News Index & Abstracts*, for example, offers a comprehensive, day-by-day summary of all news reported by the major television networks. This resource is heavily used in descriptive research on the media, but, like other familiar collections of published messages, its potential as a sampling frame for experimental materials has not been exploited.

Broadcast messages are sometimes recoverable through search of published summaries, but can also be found in public collections. For example, the University of Oklahoma houses the Kanter Political Commercial Archive, a collection of political advertisements covering all levels of American politics from the very first uses of television in campaigns to the most recent.

Even ordinary conversational interaction can be sampled from collections. One large collection is housed by the Department of Communication at the University of Texas. The collection consists of a large number of ordinary conversations, tape-recorded in natural settings, many of which have been transcribed in a detailed form suitable for research purposes. It has been suggested that these materials offer certain unique opportunities for manipulation of communication variables within a standardized performance made possible by the method of transcription (Hopper & Stucky, 1986).

Given a body of available messages, the researcher must obviously use good judgment in sampling. Messages of types irrelevant to the research question should obviously not be included, but of those messages considered relevant, selection should be as impartial as possible. Random selection from a pool of possibilities is both possible and desirable when the number of messages available exceeds the number required for the experiment.

Natural Contexts of Occurrence

When for any reason published messages prove unsatisfactory, an experimenter may choose to select messages observed and recorded in their "natural" contexts of occurrence. Of course most published messages are also "naturally occurring," but there is obviously a difference between taking a message from a published collection of some sort and selecting, observing, and recording such a message in its original presentation context. Sampling from natural contexts of occurrence is likely to be a very time-consuming process, compared with use of published resources, but in certain cases it may be the best way of gathering materials.

For example, if an experimenter needed a large sample of complaints, one reasonably efficient way of getting them would be to set up a recording device at the customer service departments of a large number of businesses. But since complaints do not exhaust the sorts of interactions taking place in customer service departments, the recordings would obviously have to be carefully searched for materials. My colleagues and I have typically used this method to locate arguments for study, observing and recording interactions in settings likely to involve argumentation. For example, over the past several years we have been recording dispute mediation sessions, in which a neutral mediator helps disputing parties resolve disagreements.

A researcher with a long-term interest in a certain domain will typically maintain personal collections of messages, gathered more or less haphazardly from various sources. Essays collected from newspapers and magazines, direct mail appeals, and other such messages might be collected by researchers interested in persuasion, while researchers interested in interpersonal communication might collect fictional representations of interpersonal processes or actual bits of conversation exhibiting a property of interest.

Communication performance classes (such as public speaking, argumentation, persuasive speaking, interpersonal communication skills, group discussion, and interviewing) often present the researcher with the opportunity to gather large numbers of messages of a given type at very low cost. Many classes of these sorts routinely record student performance as an instructional aid (for self-critique), and when permission can be obtained for research use of these materials, large samples are not difficult to generate. Granted, these materials are unlikely to come into the experimenter's hands in just the form required for the research purpose, but they can certainly serve as "kernel" messages to which manipulations can be applied. And while classroom performance is obviously not "naturally occurring" in the same sense as messages produced in response to an independent exigence, such performances do have the advantage of representing a wide variety of personal styles and personal interests.

Messages collected in natural contexts of occurrence may require various sorts of transformation before use in experimentation. The growth of naturalistic discourse analysis in communication has familiarized a well-developed technology for the detailed transcription of speech (see, for example, Schenkein, 1978, or Moerman, 1988), and this technology can certainly be adapted to the needs of the researcher in any particular case. Both content and oral performance characteristics can be transcribed, allowing naturalistic variation on many dimensions of messages without abandoning experimental control. Hopper and Stucky (1986) suggested the use of this technology for just the purpose described here. The level of fidelity that can be achieved with quite ordinary recording equipment and widely familiar transcribing methods will be more than adequate for the purposes of most experimentation on message variables.

"Laboratory" Production of Messages

Of course it is perfectly reasonable in many cases to generate messages of just the sort needed within a laboratory frame (as opposed to a natural context of occurrence). Messages can be generated by the researcher according to some plan, or they can be elicited from respondents recruited as research participants. Which choice is the more reasonable depends upon the particular circumstances of the research: the possibility, for example, of bias in messages produced solely by the experimenter.

In attempting to elicit messages of a particular type from naive respondents, the researcher must keep in mind that respondents may or may not respect categorical definitions and distinctions required by the research problem. For example, asked to write summaries of arguments they have had with spouses, friends, or family members, some people will simply insist that they never have arguments, or will offer descriptions of interactions that no one else would recognize as argumentative. Asked to recall a situation in which someone tried to persuade them to do something they did not want to do, some of them will supply situations in which they themselves took the role of persuader or in which their partner did something unpleasant without any particular persuasive intent. It should not be assumed that all messages produced in response to a set of instructions will in fact fit the category or categories of interest. Messages produced in response to experimenter's instructions will often require evaluation for fit with a category, either by the experimenter, or by independent judges.

Naturally, instructions given to respondents on what to produce should not themselves be a source of bias. When respondents are asked to write messages of a given type, and different subgroups write different types, the experimenter can subtly bias the message sample by the variations in the instructions. For example, if threats and promises are needed for the experiment, asking some respondents to supply threats and some to supply promises opens the possibility of bias in the attitude toward each category expressed by the experimenter. A better strategy might be to give uniform instructions to all of the respondents (say, to come up with a way of getting someone to do some particular thing) and to sort the responses afterwards into categories including promises and threats. If awareness of the experimental expectation might introduce bias, the experimenter ought to avoid revealing that expectation. For example, to generate experimental messages for a comparison of one-sided and two-sided argument, it might be better not to describe the contrast to respondents and then have them write two versions of their messages, but to first elicit kernel messages and then introduce the sidedness variation.

In general, all of the routine precautions taken in experimentation on humans should be extended to procedures aimed at eliciting messages. This means: (1) recognizing that the responses produced may or may not correspond with the intentions of the experimenter (so that manipulation checks may need to be incorporated into the research plan); (2) recognizing that the experimenter's expectations may affect response (and that care should be taken to avoid communicating those expectations); and (3) recognizing that "instructions" given to respondents amount to constraints on the domain sampled (so that it may often be better to elicit messages in response to representative communication situations than to elicit messages in response to an abstract description of a category).

Examples of methods for eliciting messages from respondents abound in the research literature, but usually as a basis for response measurement rather than as a basis for construction of experimental materials to be presented to new respondents. Many studies of individual differences in communication strategy, style, and skill use hypothetical tasks to stimulate the production of messages of specific kinds. For example, Clark and Delia (1977) presented grade-school children with several different problems in persuasion, in the form of imagined situations like persuading a parent to allow the child to have an overnight birthday party or persuading a stranger to take in a stray puppy. For an experimenter's purposes, a wider variety of situations would obviously be preferable. Sillars (1980) had every respondent recall some situation involving a conflict with a roommate and report on the interaction that occurred in this situation. Such an elicitation method combines a sampling of situations with a sampling of messages.

O'Keefe and McCornack's (1987) study, described earlier in this chapter, used essentially the same elicitation methods, but instead of treating the elicited methods as responses to be coded and related to other individual difference variables, O'Keefe and McCornack treated the elicited messages as experimental messages to be presented to "receivers" for response. My point here is not that one use of these research strategies is superior to the other, but only that experimentation on message variables can exploit techniques invented for other research purposes. In particular, laboratory procedures for eliciting messages of various sorts are already quite familiar, even though they have rarely been used for purposes of generating experimental stimuli.

SUMMARY

In this chapter we have considered the concept of a message class and the sort of task we face in trying to generalize about such a class. Essentially, most message samples will resemble "convenience samples" rather than random samples. While this condition should not be taken as an insurmountable barrier to generalization, it does call for greater attention to the rationale for any such generalization. I have proposed a strategy for justifying generalization based on a division of the generalization problem into two substeps: an inference from sample to "projected population" and an inference from "projected population" to some broader domain. The advantage of this division is that it allows us to see the need for different substantive premises at each step and to recognize distinctions between conclusions justified observationally and conclusions justified presumptively.

Two central sampling problems to be avoided were discussed. *Bias* in the message sample can be limited through methods of message construction and elicitation that are influenced as little as possible by the experimenter. *Collection/category mismatches* can be minimized through conceptual analysis of the category and choice of diverse cases within the category. The sensitivity of an effect to limitations of a sample can be evaluated through comparisons among several different samples, each relatively homogeneous, or through subset analysis within a single diverse sample. Plausible arguments for representativeness of a sample or for appropriateness of a sample to the sort of conclusion offered can be found in resources other than random sampling procedures.

The practical problem of generating messages for an experiment was also discussed. One practical method of generating messages for experiments is to select them from published cases or collections. Another is to collect them from their natural contexts of occurrence. A third is to construct messages under "laboratory" conditions, that is, by personally composing them or instructing respondents to compose them.

EIGHT

Method, Burden of Proof and Empirical Arguments about Message Effects

A particular view of social scientific method is evident in the preceding chapters. This view of method shapes the formulation of methodological problems as well as the development and defense of proposed solutions. The purpose of this concluding chapter is to lay out more explicitly this underlying methodological stance.

The central premise of my position is that the task of any researcher is to build a case for an empirical claim and to defend it against substantive rival views. The task of the methodologist—if such a role exists apart from concrete problem contexts—is to systematize lines of argument and counterargument peculiar to particular classes of empirical claims. Empirical claims are seen as situated within ongoing discourse organized in a fashion close to what Toulmin (1958) seems to have had in mind in speaking of "argument fields."' For convenience, I will term this general methodological stance *the argumentative view of method.*

In earlier essays (Jackson, 1986; 1989) I have contrasted the argumentative view with foundationalist and conventionalist views, both of which take method to be a set of rules for the proper conduct of scientific inquiry. A foundationalist stance toward methodology takes scientific procedures as guarantors of correct conclusions, or in weaker versions, as maximizers of correctness or minimizers of error.

Foundationalists evaluate research procedures in terms of their ability to secure the foundations of knowledge claims. Recall the discussion of the foundationalist critique of the form of statistical analysis advocated in Chapter 5. A conventionalist stance toward methodology takes scientific procedures as those rules for decisions that are commonly accepted within a community of experts. A conventionalist sees method as relative to theory and claims as relative to method.

The view proposed here is that method is neither a guarantor of correct conclusions nor a set of decision rules accepted within a community, but an analysis of the burden of proof implicit in any conclusion—the *issues* that must be addressed in any defense of an empirical claim. Methodology thus has to do with argumentative problems that accompany empirical claims; its products are strategies for generating empirical arguments. Specific research procedures are regarded here as routinized (or routinizable) solutions to argumentative problems, not as practices definitive of science itself. This view of method differs from the other views most sharply in treating procedural rules as being standard but substitutable lines of argument and the products of a deeper generative structure, which may also generate alternative procedures for specific research problems.

Concretely, what does it mean to speak of methodology as an analysis of the burden of proof associated with a class of claims? An exemplar for what I have in mind can be found in a generally acknowledged classic of social science methodology, Campbell and Stanley's (1963) monograph on experimental design. Beginning with an analysis of what is entailed by any causal claim about social processes, the monograph offers an abstract analysis of the burden of proof imposed by any such claim. The threats to internal and external validity inventoried in its opening pages are not merely a catalog of standard counterclaims (to be supplemented by other categories of threats such as those introduced in Chapter 2 of this book), but also exemplars of an analytic approach. This analytic approach involves searching the circumstances of a set of observations for any explanation that might compete with the explanatory claim that has been offered or that we wish to offer. The specific design proposals are obviously not offered as prospective research plans, but as exemplars of classes of argumentative response to the "threats." The scientific significance of this monograph is to be found in its systematic attention to strategies for satisfying a specifiable, contextualized burden of proof.

Developing an experimental methodology appropriate to message effects research requires the same sort of attention to argument and counterargument concerning causal claims about messages. Only attention to argumentative context can inform our decisions about what evidence to gather and what evidence to present.

The most important implication of this argumentative view is that method is subordinated to aim and claim—to the purpose of the research and the substantive import of the conclusions drawn from the research. All of what has been suggested in this book presupposes a characteristic aim behind message-related experiments and a characteristic form of empirical claim. The aim might be briefly described as evaluation of message effects, often with an underlying practical interest in strategic choice or improvement of performance. The characteristic claims are comparisons among message classes or among strategic options. The burden of proof involved in experiments on message variables is limited by these features of the research, and responsiveness to this contextualized burden of proof is the key to development of an adequate methodology for message research.

From the argumentative point of view, the most important thing to be learned from the study of methods is not a collection of procedures for doing research, but a core set of issues that regularly arise in the defense of certain classes of empirical claims—stock issues of a sort. This does not, of course, mean that procedures are unimportant, since most of the time procedures associated with a particular mode of research are tailored for responsiveness to the underlying issues. What it means is that procedures are subordinate to issues, and that they may be replaced with other procedures that offer other ways of responding to the issues.

As might be anticipated, the consequences of adopting an argumentative view of method are extremely far-reaching. Although this book has been concerned with a single cluster of methodological problems, it should be plain that the argumentative view of method represents a very general stance toward the nature of empirical research and the status of its products. This stance will have practical implications for many methodological problems and controversies beyond those addressed here. In the next section, I will outline some of these implications, and in the final section I will return to the problem of analyzing the burden of proof involved in making claims about message effects.

CONSEQUENCES OF VIEWING METHOD AS ARGUMENTATIVE

I take the three most fundamental consequences of the argumentative view to be these: (1) a turn toward "plausible reasoning" as the standard for scientific argumentation; (2) an emphasis on burden of proof as a generative mechanism in empirical argumentation; and (3) a recognition of the limitations of design in the construction of an empirical case.

Plausible Reasoning

In argumentation theory, it is common to differentiate between demonstrative and nondemonstrative argument, and also common to think of the former as the model for scientific argumentation and the latter as the model for practical decision making in contexts of uncertainty (see, e.g., Ehninger, 1970). However, contemporary studies of science call into doubt the association of scientific reasoning with demonstrative argument (see, e.g., Finocchario, 1980; Franklin, 1989; Kuhn, 1962; Laudan, 1984; Nelson, McGill, & McCloskey, 1987; Nickles, 1989; Polya, 1954; Rescher, 1976). The interdisciplinary "rhetoric of science" movement embodies a pervasive contemporary view of science as being concerned with issues that are always, inherently, and indefinitely arguable.

To suppose that science is simply demonstrative is hardly tenable, but scientists nevertheless often resist the idea that science is a rhetorical process in which argumentation is not merely a distortion but an essential component. The basis for this resistance may be a simple failure to envision any alternative scientific ethic. Communication theorists writing for a recently published project on "paradigm dialogues" argued that scientists should act as though engaged in demonstrative argument because striving for demonstrativeness is the distinguishing feature of science: "It is this striving that differentiates scientific methods of information gathering and evaluation from other types" (Cappella, 1989, p. 142). To give up the demonstrative ideal seems to some scientists tantamount to giving up science itself.

The position taken here and in much contemporary theorizing about knowledge is that rationality inheres not in forms of demonstration but in discourse processes. Science has the credibility and success that it does, not because it restricts itself to certain observational practices and certain argumentative forms, but because it is built on certain norms of discourse—two in particular: public expression of doubt and accountability to critique. In practice, scientists have never succeeded in conclusively *demonstrating* anything to be true, but they have achieved useful consensus about many, many questions of fact. They do so not by striving for—and certainly not by achieving—a demonstrative ideal, but by working through the alternatives available, given the problem context, the current conceptions of the science's objectives, and the current conceptualizations of the subject matter. Scientists cannot, of course, rule out alternatives they cannot envision, and hence cannot ever be sure that their current beliefs are "justified" in the epistemological foundationalists' sense of that term. But when no alternatives to a current belief can be envisioned, it is not clear what, if anything, is gained by pointing out that we cannot be absolutely sure the belief is true.

Assuming a basic readiness to abandon demonstrativeness as a standard, we must search for some other idealization of scientific reasoning. One alternative is to see scientific method as argumentative, and to adopt a view of scientific argument that recognizes its embeddedness in empirical controversies. To see method in this way means that attention is drawn to what is being claimed and to the evaluation of evidence in relation to what is being claimed. In other words, evidence is evaluated not for its ability to "verify" a claim (in the foundationalist sense of verification), but for its ability to guide choice among alternative positions.

Research is always purposeful (whether the purpose be choice among practical actions or choice among alternative possible beliefs), and the purpose will generally constrain what might in principle amount to an infinite set of alternatives. Good science will involve strong arguments—not necessarily conclusive arguments, but arguments that exclude competing claims and answer relevant sorts of objections. Of course such arguments will also appeal to facts, and they will respond to the challenges posed by facts.

Nondemonstrative arguments that are nevertheless worthy of acceptance have been studied under the label "plausible reasoning" (Polya, 1954; Rescher, 1976). All induction falls into the category of nondemonstrative argument, unless we cheat by building an inferential rule into the argument itself as a premise offered without any possibility of defense. Arguments that take a deductive form but use premises that must be justified inductively are also nondemonstrative. Virtually all actual scientific argument fits one of these nondemonstrative types, so the consequence of adopting the argumentative view of method is not to change scientific practice but to change the justification offered for scientific practice. The difference between the foundationalist and argumentative views is partly reflected in a difference between treating plausible reasoning as an imperfect approximation of demonstrative reasoning and treating plausible reasoning as itself an idealization of research practice.

What sorts of practices are suggested by what we know of plausible reasoning? Perhaps most important for my purposes in this book has been the willingness to operate from reasonable presumptions and the willingness to treat a strong presumption as a virtual conclusion. Consider the important problem of arguing for the generality of a treatment effect across a population of persons or across a category of messages. I have proposed a strategy for building a presumption of generality based on some limited number of demonstrations of insensitivity to contextual variation.

There is nothing original in this proposal—scientists do this all the time—but there is some novelty, perhaps, in the association of the strategy with a systematic methodological viewpoint. Such a strategy would be of no use to someone truly committed to foundationalism as either an epistemological or a methodological position, for evidence that an effect is insensitive to *some* contextual variations is obviously no sort of guarantee that it is insensitive to all such variations. Within an argumentative view, an effect proposed as general can be entertained as a sort of presumption if accompanied by evidence that it is reliable in the face of varying conditions, with the strength of the presumption increasing as the evidence of insensitivity to contextual variables becomes more extensive and more varied.

Burden of Proof

The argumentative view of method differs from other views of method in what it takes to be the generative basis for scientific argument. "Rule-bound methodologies" (McCloskey, 1985) take scientific procedures to be the generative basis for scientific work, which is to say that they assume that to do science is simply to follow a certain set of accepted rules for observation and analysis. The difference between my view and these others can be partially described in terms of the differing obligations we would place on the researcher. Their views emphasize procedures: specifically, procedures accepted within a community of experts as offering a good chance of producing correct conclusions. My view deemphasizes procedures and draws attention instead to the underlying issues that the procedures respond to; that is, to burden of proof as a generative mechanism for empirical arguments.

To clarify what is meant by "burden of proof" in the present context, it is an argumentative, and not an epistemological, construct. It refers not to abstract, universal requirements for knowing, but to what a researcher is committed to believing and defending by virtue of having made a claim of a certain kind. For any class of substantive claims, some partially specifiable class of rivals will be implicit, and the defense of a claim will always be centered on responding to these rivals. Burden of proof depends upon the capacity of the field, the community, or the culture to envision alternatives to the claim being made; it is bound not to issues of justification, in the epistemological sense, but to issues of choice between alternative theoretical claims or alternative courses of action.

An important point often neglected in methodological writing is that empirical claims differ one from another, and that as claims differ, so do the issues that might bear on the acceptability of the claims. Seeing methodology as concerned with argumentation has as a corollary a view of research itself as a case-building process. The kind of case that must be built depends on the kind of claim being defended. Thus, any specifiable empirical claim will involve an analyzable burden of proof, but that burden of proof will vary with the nature of the claim. The adequacy of any experiment cannot be judged independently of the substantive import of the claim; adequacy of an empirical argument is strictly a function of whether or not it satisfies its own contextually determined burden of proof.

We can differentiate within current communication research many fundamentally distinct classes of claims, each imposing a distinctive burden of proof. We can differentiate, for example, descriptive generalizations from causal claims. Among causal claims, we can further differentiate between "can cause" claims (concerned with the abstract possibility of bringing about Y by manipulating X in the right circumstances) and "does cause" claims (concerned with what can normally be expected from a manipulation of X).[1] Many of the claims we are most concerned with in this book are best described as "does cause" claims: assertions about what effects can be expected given some sort of variation in type of message or in message characteristics. However, even among "does cause" claims, important differences arise from the substantive problem context.

The burden of proof associated with any individual claim is only partly analyzable in terms of the abstract features of its class. It will also depend on substantive beliefs about the phenomena studied, and perhaps too on the particulars of the problem and research purpose. Regardless of subject matter, it is common to regard causal claims as sharing a common core of subordinate commitments: It seems clear that to claim that X causes Y commits the researcher to a belief that both X and Y vary, to a belief in the nonspurious association of X and Y, and to a belief in the temporal precedence of X. However, this is by no means sufficient to define the burden of proof associated with causal claims about a subject matter (such as message effects). Even if we differentiate among causal claims, giving separate analyses for claims about necessary causes, sufficient causes, and causes that are neither necessary nor sufficient, we would still be unable to give a full account of the burden of proof associated with a claim about message effects, because to specify abstractly what is meant by the claim is not to delineate the issues that are, relative to the subject matter, truly problematic.

Recall the discussion in Chapter 1 of the relationship between experimental methods and causal claims. Experimentation as a general research strategy is tailored to a very general burden of proof inherent in a causal claim, but placed into any concrete problem context this general burden of proof is reshaped. The burden of proof involved in causal claims about human behavior depends upon and changes with substantive knowledge—substantive knowledge not only about behavior, but also about the properties of experiments on human behavior. Social scientists simply take for granted that experiments on social phenomena require observation of many people, so as to deal with the problem of human idiosyncrasy. Likewise, they recognize the need for double-blind procedures to handle the problem of human expectancy. These issues play no part in experimentation in other fields where the materials experimented on lack expectations and individuality.

There is an important point to be taken about the burden of proof associated with causal claims about human behavior: It has changed over time as we have learned about our objects of study (Laudan, 1984). Certain design features now taken very much for granted (such as randomization of replications and double-blind procedures) are 20th-century inventions (Gigenrenzer et al., 1989). These design features, invented to respond to underlying issues of variability and expectancy, had to emerge from the practice of experimentation, specifically, from claim and counterclaim, critique and response. An argumentative position acknowledges the possibility that we do not necessarily know all of the ways experiments on human behavior (or other phenomena) can go wrong, but it demands that we respond to what we do know can go wrong. The burden of proof associated with any class of claims is partly "field independent" in Toulmin's (1958) sense, but also partly "field dependent," and unspecifiable apart from substantive problem context.

If the burden of proof is not specifiable apart from substantive problem context, how do we know what it is? That is a question for foundationalists, one that is not quite meaningful from within the argumentative view. The burden of proof is simply a matter of responding to what we can currently envision of alternatives to our proposed interpretations of data. Burden of proof is dependent on what questions and objections can be anticipated in response to an empirical claim, and this is always embedded in a social and historical context characterized by a "present level of understanding" within a field. Issues that are inaccessible to us at our current level of conceptual progress must be allowed to emerge as they always have, through someone noticing something that is not quite as it should be or someone offering a novel interpretation of a set of facts. This book has been framed explicitly as an effort to redefine the burden of proof associated with claims about message effects, by outlining the form of some counterclaims that can be pressed against certain empirical arguments.

We progress in the complexity of the claims we make, and we progress in our understandings of our objects of study. Since burden of proof is embedded in both of these things, the burden of proof taken on in making claims about messages should be assumed to change over time, for the most part getting more and more difficult to meet.

The Limitations of "Design" in Empirical Argument

The last implication of the argumentative view to be considered here returns to a point alluded to earlier: the diminished position awarded to procedures. Good procedures do not guarantee good conclusions. One reason for this is that the burden of proof associated with a claim is not always the mirror image of the burden of proof associated with its alternatives.

Research design involves planning a set of observations so as to permit the building of a strong case for an answer to a research question. However, design decisions usually reflect some sort of expectation about the outcome of the research and some judgment as to where the presumption rests. A design well suited to meeting the burden of proof associated with the expected answer may permit only a partial or tentative defense of alternative answers.

This is a familiar enough point for those trained in the logic of statistical hypothesis testing. If an experiment is designed to demonstrate a relationship between two variables, the failure of the experiment does not ordinarily satisfy the burden of proof associated with arguing for the absence of any relationship. Thus, good design and procedure do not always underwrite strong conclusions. Good design may produce weak argumentation if the researcher ends up advancing a claim different from the one the research set out to warrant, and poor design may produce strong argument if the researcher gets lucky.

This point emphasizes once again the difference between methodology as a set of guidelines for correct performance and methodology as an analytic mentality and intellectual commitment. We cannot separate the design of the study from the conclusions drawn from it; we should not say that the study was "well done" but the conclusions unjustified. The design of an individual study can only be evaluated relative to the claim advanced, and likewise, general design prototypes can only be evaluated relative to a class of claims to be advanced.

An argumentative view locates "validity" in the relationship between conclusions and evidence, not in designs and procedures. Common ways of talking about research design reflect a very general supposition that validity is a feature of the procedures themselves: To speak, for example, of an "internally invalid" experimental design or of a "validated" measure of communicative competence is to assign validity to procedure without regard for what is to be claimed (see also D. O'Keefe, 1987). The argumentative view of method emphasizes that issues of validity can only be assessed with respect to conclusions, and then only when the entire case in support of a conclusion is considered.

ARGUING CLAIMS ABOUT MESSAGE EFFECTS

Understanding the structure of an empirical argument requires a basic differentiation between support and refutation. Support refers to the reasons that can be given for believing that a claim is true, and refutation to the reasons that can be given for rejecting challenges or alternatives to the claim. The support for a claim about message effects will be some sort of evidence that the message variable of interest covaries with the outcome of interest. But such support is not ordinarily sufficient, for one can challenge it as spurious or supplant it with a rival hypothesis. The refutational components of an empirical argument about message effects respond to these challenges and rivals.

We can reconstruct any actual empirical argument as representing at least two general standpoints, the first being the standpoint expressed in the claim, and the second being the standpoint of an imagined antagonist. The refutations incorporated into an empirical argument depend upon the imagined antagonist, that is, on the researcher's ability to turn a critical perspective on his or her own claim and to anticipate counterarguments. The evidence put forward in support of a claim will follow from what it is the researcher takes to be problematic, when the claim is viewed from the standpoint of the antagonist. Thus, experiments and other forms of empirical inquiry are structured by the antagonistic viewpoint envisioned by the researcher or, in other words, by the set of issues the researcher expects to have raised against the empirical claim. There is an imagined antagonist behind the structure of unreplicated categorical comparisons and unreplicated treatment comparisons, and a different imagined antagonist behind the structure of replicated experiments. The difference between these two model antagonists is in what challenges they raise against claims about message effects. An unreplicated treatment comparison, for example, answers a less skeptical antagonist than does a replicated treatment comparison: The unreplicated design treats as unproblematic the isolability of the treatment variable and the stability of the treatment from message to message, while the replicated design recognizes that these may be in doubt and generates data to answer this doubt.

Any given component of an empirical argument may serve either as support or as refutation of a possible objection. This separation of functions, support and refutation, is quite important in evaluating empirical arguments, because evidence and reasoning that are insufficient to support a claim may well be sufficient to refute some counterclaim. Argumentative components aimed at answering refutations must be responsive to those refutations, but they need not suffice as independent support for a broader claim. We have seen how arguments over the validity of statistical procedures may turn on the distinction between results presented as support for a claim and results presented as responsive to a possible refutation. The "foundationalist" critique of treating messages as "random" considers the statistical outcomes as support for claims about message classes, while the methodological perspective advocated here considers statistical outcomes as data used to refute a certain class of challenges in principle to claims about message classes based on observation of concrete cases.

I argued earlier, in Chapter 1, that support for a claim about message effects must incorporate evidence of covariation between the message variable and the outcome variable. This is, I think, uncontroversial. Such evidence is, of course, disputable, but if there is anything uniquely disputable about the measurement of covariation between message variables and outcome variables, it has not yet come to my attention. However, even where the covariation itself is not disputed, the case for any claim about the dependency of the outcome on the message variable must also include refutations of competing *accounts* of the covariation. These competing accounts are the points of controversy to which the data must be made to respond. They define the major components of the researcher's burden of proof.

The specific proposals for design and analysis outlined in this book are intended as possible responses to these standard points of controversy. The purpose of including replications in an experiment is to produce data needed to answer one sort of objection. The purpose of treating replications as random is to avoid another set of objections. And the purpose of certain precautions taken in "sampling" messages is to answer still another set of objections. Let us spell these out as explicitly as possible, by considering a typical claim about message effects and the sorts of questions and challenges that might be raised by an idealized antagonist.

We will take as our example claim the following statement: Two-sided argumentation is more persuasive than one-sided argumentation. The support for this claim will be some sort of evidence of covariation between sidedness and persuasiveness, presumably based on a comparison of audience response to one-sided messages and audience response to two-sided messages. What questions and objections might be raised against such a claim? What reasons might an antagonist have for rejecting such a claim? We can list at least three broad classes of objections, as follows:

1. Sidedness has no systematic effect on persuasiveness, but some case-specific effect for every message that depends on particulars of content. The covariation observed in the messages observed is only what would be expected as a result of unsystematic case-to-case fluctuations in the apparent advantage of sidedness. This is essentially an attack on the *evidence* of covariation, and it is a question that is normally answered through use of inferential statistics.

2. The outcome variation observed is not the result of differences in sidedness, but the result of differences in some other message feature. This objection can come in two forms: a charge that some specific other variable is confounded with sidedness, or a charge that there is no protection against an indefinite set of possible confounds. This class of objections has to do with the *interpretation* of the covariation.

3. The effect observed within this experiment is not generalizable beyond a certain limited category of messages. This objection does not necessarily challenge the validity of the claim within its limited domain, but may, in some cases, point to so narrow a domain as to make the claim uninteresting. If we will refer to the first class of objections as having to do with the *evidence* of covariation, and to the second as having to do with the *interpretation* of covariation, we can refer to the third class of objections as having to do with the *scope* or *domain* of the relationship.

Including message replications in experiments on message variables is, in the vast majority of research situations, a practical precondition for responding to all three issues. However, its fundamental rationale is to be found in the questions of interpretation. The central purpose of including replications is to avoid a complete confounding of sidedness with other noticed or unnoticed influences on persuasiveness. Random variations in the quality of individual messages threaten unreplicated designs, but not replicated designs. Systematic association of the variable of interest (sidedness) with other variables (such as length) cannot be avoided mechanically in either replicated or unreplicated designs, but can be more easily noticed within a replicated design and (unless the confounding is complete) can be evaluated post hoc within a replicated design.

Treating messages as random is an answer to the first set of issues, the questions of evidence. There are obviously many other ways to answer such a question (all of which are, however, equally dependent on having observed many cases). The treatment of messages as random is not intended as an answer to the questions of scope (as Morley, 1988, seemed to suppose), nor is it intended as an answer to the questions of evidence (as Hunter et al., 1989, seemed to suppose). Treating messages as random does not guarantee freedom from confounding, nor does it guarantee generalizability to any sort of "message population," but it does answer the first objection listed above, by discounting the observed treatment effect by an amount consistent with the assumptions of the objection. Quite obviously, this analytic strategy can be replaced by other strategies similar in spirit: One might, for example, apply meta-analysis techniques to existing bodies of unreplicated experiments, or conduct message-by-message analysis that is later integrated into some sort of generalized claim.

The questions of scope or domain can be attacked in various ways, depending on the research question and the particular circumstances of the research. One way is through use of a sampling plan that offers a satisfactory representation of the domain of interest. Another way is through development of a presumption of generality. Earlier I suggested that one way to do this is to try to show that an effect is insensitive to certain circumstantial variations that might reasonably be suspected of "moderating" the effect. For example, we might argue for the generality of a sidedness effect by showing that two-sided argumentation is superior to one-sided argumentation, not only for audiences unfavorable to the speaker's claim but also for audiences favorable to it, not only for high-credibility speakers but also for low-credibility speakers, not only for educated audiences but also for uneducated audiences, and so on. This strategy is already extremely common in meta-analysis of social research; it is an argumentative strategy closely parallel to forms of plausible reasoning in mathematics, as described by Polya (1954). Note the profound difference between these two ways of arguing generality: One depends on showing that there is an average effect within a domain, despite whatever variation there might be in the effect, and the other depends on showing that various ways of partitioning the domain would not change our conclusion about the effect.

What would a strong argument in support of a claim about message effects look like? The viewpoint represented in the earlier chapters of this book is that a strong argument for such a claim will offer answers or rebuttals to a series of specific questions and challenges, to include (among more general issues) the three issues listed above. A strong argument can answer these issues in any number of ways, so it should not be supposed that experiments on message effects must always have some one canonical form. To take the specific design and analysis strategies advocated in this book as the only proper way to conduct such experiments is to entirely miss my point. A researcher's task is to *confront the issues*, not to jump through a certain number of hoops set up by a textbook writer or a dissertation committee or a journal editor. How these issues are confronted depends on the resources at hand and the creativity of the individual in making use of them.

I have tried to stress throughout this book that arguments mapped out abstractly cannot substitute for particularized analysis of individual empirical arguments. Issues developed here as threats to validity or constraints on generalizability are not "design errors" whose presence invalidates a conclusion. They are basic lines of argument, intended as much to help the producers of a study to anticipate counterarguments as to help consumers of the study to evaluate its claims. Finding invalidity in an empirical argument is a matter of identifying substantive rival hypotheses rather than a matter of comparing an experiment to a set of required design features and counting off its "good" and "bad" points.

This book has been as much concerned with defining the *issues* to which empirical arguments will be addressed as with describing strategies for building the arguments themselves. The development of communication research methodology must ultimately depend on what issues can be made controversial within the framework of our theoretical assumptions about our objects of study. The experience of the past suggests that we can never exhaust the issues that need to be addressed, but can only confront them as they arise in the context of specific theoretical and empirical controversies. This should clarify the intent behind the book: The critique of current research practice is intended to make controversial what has so far been presumed nonproblematic, and the suggestions about design and analysis are intended as plans for arguing and counterarguing within this newly constructed context of controversy.

Expected Mean Squares for Selected Designs

The general problems associated with analysis of experiments incorporating replication factors are addressed in any good handbook on the analysis of variance, either in discussion of random factors or in discussion of mixed-model analysis of variance (e.g., Glass & Hopkins, 1984; Keppel, 1982; Winer, 1971). The purpose of this Appendix is not to duplicate these discussions but to amplify the reasoning behind analyses recommended in Chapters 3 and 4.

To make appropriate choices of F tests in any experimental arrangement it is necessary to examine the expected mean squares for each effect within the design. Easily applied algorithms for generating expected mean squares may be found in any of the texts mentioned above.

For the purposes of this Appendix and related material in the text, individual observations will be denoted as X with subscripts used to index the conditions under which the observations are made. In a one-factor design, an individual observation would be denoted X_{ij}, to indicate the jth observation within the ith level of the factor. In a two-factor design, an individual observation would be denoted X_{ijk}, to indicate the kth observation taken within the ijth cell. Nesting of the levels of one factor under the levels of another is indicated by a slash following the subscript representing the nested factor. In every case, we must begin with a statistical model of the individual score that points to the sources of variation in scores. Every design implies a different model of the individual score.

Design 1: *Message replications nested under classes, and persons nested under messages (see Figure 3.2).*

This design, identical to what Winer (1971) terms a hierarchical nested design, implies the following model of the individual score.

$$X_{ijk} = \mu + \kappa_i + \gamma_{j/i} + \epsilon_{k/ij}$$

where:

μ is the population mean score;

κ_i is the effect associated with category i;

$\gamma_{j/i}$ is the effect associated with replication j within category i; and

$\epsilon_{k/ij}$ is the unique error term associated with the kth observation related to the jth replication within category i.

When the replications are considered levels of a random factor (i.e., replaceable with an indefinitely large number of equally acceptable examples from the class of interest), this model gives rise to expected mean squares shown in Table A.1.

To test differences among the classes, find a mean square that would be equal to the class mean square if the null hypothesis were true (i.e., if the variance among the class effects were equal to zero). In this case, the appropriate error term for testing the class effect is the messages-within-class mean square, since if the "null hypothesis component," σ_κ^2, is set to zero, the expected values of MS_C and $MS_{M/C}$ would be equal.

Design 2: *Persons nested within classes, and message replications nested within persons (see Figure 3.3).*

This design differs from the first only in which random factor is nested under the other. However, since it is now possible to estimate

TABLE A.1. Expected Mean Squares for Design 1

Source	Expected mean squares
Class	$mn\sigma_\kappa^2 + n\sigma_\gamma^2 + \sigma_\epsilon^2$
Messages/class	$n\sigma_\gamma^2 + \sigma_\epsilon^2$
Persons/messages	σ_ϵ^2

Note. m is the number of replications per class, and *n* is the number of persons per cell.

TABLE A.2. Expected Mean Squares for Design 2

Source	Expected mean squares
Class	$mn\sigma_\kappa^2 + m\sigma_\pi^2 + \sigma_\gamma^2 + \sigma_\epsilon^2$
Persons/class	$m\sigma_\pi^2 + \sigma_\gamma^2 + \sigma_\epsilon^2$
Messages/persons	$\sigma_\gamma^2 + \sigma_\epsilon^2$

Note. n is the number of persons per class, and *m* is the number of replications per person.

the "person" effect separately from error, the underlying model is somewhat different in appearance.

$$X_{ijk} = \mu + \kappa_i + \pi_{j/i} + \gamma_{k/ij} + \epsilon_{ijk}$$

where $\pi_{j/i}$ is the "person" effect, all else as before.

It should be noted that although there is no way to obtain separate estimates of $\gamma_{k/ij}$ and ϵ_{ijk} (or of σ_γ^2 and σ_ϵ^2), there is no harm in drawing a conceptual distinction between these sources of variation, and doing so has the advantage of showing where replication-related variance appears in such a design. Expected mean squares for this design are shown in Table A.2.

As should be apparent here, the *F* test required to evaluate class differences is formed using the persons-within-classes mean square.

Design 3: *Message replications nested within classes, persons crossed with both classes and messages (see Figure 3.5).*

The sort of design considered here comes about when each person responds to each replication within each class, making both class and replications repeated or within-subjects factors. The statistical model implied by this design is as follows.

$$X_{ijk} = \mu + \kappa_i + \gamma_{j/i} + \pi_k + \kappa\pi_{ik} + \gamma\pi_{jk/i} + \epsilon_{ijk}$$

where:

$\kappa\pi_{ik}$ represents the class × person interaction;

$\gamma\pi_{jk/i}$ represents the replication × person interaction; and as before,

ϵ_{ijk}, though presumed present, cannot be estimated separately.

TABLE A.3. Expected Mean Squares for Design 3

Source	Expected mean squares
Class	$mn\sigma_\kappa^2 + n\sigma_\gamma^2 + m\sigma_{\kappa\pi}^2 + \sigma_{\gamma\pi}^2 + \sigma_\epsilon^2$
Messages/class	$+ n\sigma_\gamma^2 \quad\quad + \sigma_{\gamma\pi}^2 + \sigma_\epsilon^2$
Persons	$mc\sigma_\pi^2 \quad\quad\quad\quad + \sigma_{\gamma\pi}^2 + \sigma_\epsilon^2$
Class × person	$m\sigma_{\kappa\pi}^2 + \sigma_{\gamma\pi}^2 + \sigma_\epsilon^2$
Message × person	$\sigma_{\gamma\pi}^2 + \sigma_\epsilon^2$

Note. c is the number of classes, *m* is the number of replications per class, and *n* is the total number of persons.

Examining the expected mean squares arrayed in Table A.3, it becomes clear that to test the class effect requires a quasi *F* ratio, formed by combining mean squares to create composites in the numerator and denominator that differ only in the null hypothesis component σ_κ^2. Besides the quasi *F* ratio shown in the text of Chapter 3, it would be possible to test the class effect with the ratio

$$F' = MS_C/(MS_{M/C} + MS_{P\times C} - MS_{P\times M/C}).$$

Design 4: *Message replications and persons nested within class, but crossed with one another (see Figure 3.6).*

This sort of design comes about when each person responds to all of the replications within a single class, but not to the replications within other classes. Expected mean squares for this design appear in Table A.4.

TABLE A.4. Expected Mean Squares for Design 4

Source	Expected mean squares
Class	$mn\sigma_\kappa^2 + n\sigma_\gamma^2 + m\sigma_\pi^2 + \sigma_{\gamma\pi}^2 + \sigma_\epsilon^2$
Messages/class	$n\sigma_\gamma^2 \quad\quad + \sigma_{\gamma\pi}^2 + \sigma_\epsilon^2$
Persons/class	$m\sigma_\pi^2 + \sigma_{\gamma\pi}^2 + \sigma_\epsilon^2$
Messages × persons	$\sigma_{\gamma\pi}^2 + \sigma_\epsilon^2$

Note. c is the number of classes, *m* is the number of message replications per class, *n* is the number of persons per class, and *mn* is the number of observations per class.

An appropriate quasi F test for the class effect can be constructed as described in Chapter 3 or, alternatively, as follows.

$$F' = MS_C/(MS_{M/C} + MS_{P/C} - MS_{M \times P/C})$$

Design 5: *Message replications crossed with treatments, persons nested in treatment* × *message cells (see Figure 4.1).*

This is a standard independent groups factorial design; it comes about when replications are matched across levels of the treatment variable, and each person receives only one replication at one level of the treatment variable. Using τ_i to represent the effect associated with the ith treatment, γ_j as before to represent the replication effect, and $\tau\gamma_{ij}$ to represent the treatment × replication interaction, the model implied by this design is as follows:

$$X_{ijk} = \mu + \tau_i + \gamma_j + \tau\gamma_{ij} + \epsilon_{ijk}$$

Expected mean squares for this design appear in Table A.5. The F test for the treatment effect uses as an error term not the within-groups mean square, but the treatment × message mean square, as a consequence of the replication factor being considered random.

Design 6: *Treatments crossed with message replications, persons nested under treatments but crossed with replications (see Figure 4.3).*

This repeated measures design comes about when each person responds to all of the messages subjected to a given treatment. The model implied by this design is as follows:

TABLE A.5. Expected Mean Squares for Design 5

Source	Expected mean squares
Treatments	$mn\sigma_\tau^2 \quad + n\sigma_{\tau\gamma}^2 + \sigma_\epsilon^2$
Messages	$tn\sigma_\gamma^2 \quad + \sigma_\epsilon^2$
Treatment × message	$+n\sigma_{\tau\gamma}^2 + \sigma_\epsilon^2$
Persons/groups	σ_ϵ^2

Note. t is the number of treatments, m is the number of replications, and n is the number of persons per cell.

TABLE A.6. Expected Mean Squares for Design 6

Source	Expected mean squares
Treatments	$mn\sigma_\tau^2 \qquad + m\sigma_\pi^2 + n\sigma_{\gamma\tau}^2 + \sigma_{\gamma\pi}^2 + \sigma_\epsilon^2$
Messages	$tn\sigma_\gamma^2 \qquad\qquad\qquad + \sigma_{\gamma\pi}^2 + \sigma_\epsilon^2$
Persons/treatments	$+ m\sigma_\pi^2 \qquad\qquad + \sigma_{\gamma\pi}^2 + \sigma_\epsilon^2$
Messages × treatments	$+ n\sigma_{\gamma\tau}^2 + \sigma_{\gamma\pi}^2 + \sigma_\epsilon^2$
Messages × persons	$\sigma_{\gamma\pi}^2 + \sigma_\epsilon^2$

Note. t is the number of treatments, m is the number of replications, and n is the number of persons per treatment.

$$X_{ijk} = \mu + \tau_i + \gamma_j + \pi_{k/i} + \tau\gamma_{ij} + \gamma\pi_{jk/i} + \epsilon_{ijk}$$

Expected mean squares for this design appear in Table A.6. As explained in Chapter 4, the test of the treatment effect involves a quasi F ratio.

Design 7: *Replicated factorial design with independent groups (see Figure 4.6).*

Apart from the fact that the replication factor is treated as random, this design is identical to a three-way factorial design with independent groups. Using τ to refer to effects associated with the first treatment

TABLE A.7. Expected Mean Squares for Design 7

Source	Expected mean squares
Treatments$_1$	$t'mn\sigma_\tau^2 \qquad\qquad + t'n\sigma_{\tau\gamma}^2 + \sigma_\epsilon^2$
Treatments$_2$	$tmn\sigma_\lambda^2 \qquad\qquad + tn\sigma_{\lambda\gamma}^2 + \sigma_\epsilon^2$
Treatment$_1$ × Treatment$_2$	$mn\sigma_{\tau\lambda}^2 + n\sigma_{\tau\lambda\gamma}^2 + \sigma_\epsilon^2$
Messages	$t'tn\sigma_\gamma^2 \qquad\qquad\qquad + \sigma_\epsilon^2$
Message × Treament$_1$	$+ t'n\sigma_{\tau\gamma}^2 + \sigma_\epsilon^2$
Message × Treatment$_2$	$+ tn\sigma_{\lambda\gamma}^2 + \sigma_\epsilon^2$
Message × Treatment$_1$ × Treatment$_2$	$+ n\sigma_{\tau\lambda\gamma}^2 + \sigma_\epsilon^2$
Persons/groups	σ_ϵ^2

Note. t is the number of levels of the first treatment variable; t' is the number of levels of the second treatment variable; m is the number of distinct replications; n is the number of persons within each of the $t \times t' \times m$ cells.

variable and λ to refer to effects associated with the second treatment variable, the following model is suggested:

$$X_{ijkl} = \mu + \tau_i + \lambda_j + \tau\lambda_{ij} + \gamma_k + \tau\gamma_{ik} + \lambda\gamma_{jk} + \tau\lambda\gamma_{ijk} + \epsilon_{ijkl}$$

Examining the expected mean squares in Table A.7, notice that tests of the manipulated variables and their interactions require individually tailored F ratios.

NOTES

TWO

1. An excerpt from the "high-fear" lecture appears in the research report:

If you ever develop an infection of this kind from improper care of your teeth, it will be an extremely serious matter because these infections are really dangerous. They can spread to your eyes or your heart or your joints and cause secondary infections which may lead to diseases such as arthritic paralysis, kidney damage, or total blindness.

The high-fear lecture contained 71 references to bad consequences of poor dental hygiene, ranging from pain associated with dental work to life-threatening diseases. Visual materials accompanying the lecture also varied: X-rays and diagrams used in the low-fear version were replaced with slides showing horrible examples of infections in the high-fear version.

2. Actually, things are considerably more complex than this, because for any given one-sided message, there will obviously be multiple ways to introduce two-sidedness, and these too will vary in effect. Indeed, the various versions of a "single" message can hardly be supposed to be a distinct class at all. However, the problems introduced by this complexity can be attacked in the same fashion as the problems discussed here. The simplistic view of "the message" projected by this discussion is adopted only for presentational clarity.

THREE

1. The appropriateness of treating messages as a random factor remains a controversial issue and will be discussed thoroughly in Chapter 5.

2. Designs with nested replications require special care in analysis. Standard analysis-of-variance computer programs such as those available within the SAS and SPSS systems generally assume (unless instructed otherwise) that factors are crossed rather than nested and fixed rather than random, and in some cases it may not be possible to adapt the analysis to the design employed. Alternatives in such cases are to use the standard programs to compute basic sums of squares and mean squares, completing the analysis by hand, or to shift to more specialized programs (such as SAS GLM or VARCOMP or SPSS MANOVA in place of the corresponding ANOVA programs). SAS is a registered trademark of SAS Institute Inc. SPSS is a registered trademark

of SPSS Inc. Specific programs offered through the SAS and SPSS systems (e.g., SAS ANOVA, GLM, and VARCOMP or SPSS ANOVA and MANOVA) are described in user's manuals published to support each program's operation.

3. Interested readers can consult Forster and Dickinson (1976), Santa, Miller, and Shaw (1979), and Maxwell and Bray (1986).

FOUR

1. Objections to treating messages as a random factor, including objections related to statistical power, are considered in later chapters.

2. Note the implications of this argument for procedures commonly used in meta-analysis to search for "moderator" variables. There is a great deal of difference between saying that the success of a strategy—like sidedness—depends on a moderator variable and saying that the apparent effect of a manipulation depends on the presence of a superfluous treatment. The same data might lead to either conclusion, and the plausibility of the alternative conclusions is mostly a matter of local particulars.

FIVE

1. Any good analysis-of-variance handbook will offer a general introduction to the concept of expected mean squares and some algorithm for generating expected mean squares for any given design (see, e.g., Glass & Hopkins, 1984; Keppel, 1982; Winer, 1971). Expected mean squares for fixed factors include terms that must be adjusted to yield appropriate estimates of population variance components (see Vaughan and Corballis, 1969), a complexity that will not concern us as long as we are using expected mean squares only to choose appropriate significance tests.

2. In different designs (with, say, messages nested under subjects), the same assumptions about messages would lead to different choices of error terms. Imagine, for example, that we wanted to compare the funniness of two types of jokes. Any given respondent could be observed responding to several examples of each type of joke, with jokes chosen uniquely for each person. Then individual jokes would be considered a random factor nested within both persons and joke type, and the correct error term for testing joke type would be the person × type interaction.

SIX

1. To understand this point, suppose the effect of emotionality in a persuasive message is generally positive, but somewhat variable from message to message. Five experiments conducted on the effect of emotionality each

begin with an independent kernel message, on such topics as drunk driving, drug testing for transportation workers, amateurism and professionalism in Olympic competition, environmentalism, and political correctness. If (as seems reasonable enough) some of these messages are better vehicles for an emotional appeal than others, we would expect five identically designed experiments to vary in result simply by virtue of using kernel messages varying in receptivity to an emotional appeal. When we conduct five experiments, not identically designed, but varying in audience type, dependent variable, and other details, there is no way to decide how much of the variation in outcome is related to these variations in the experiments and how much to sheer message-to-message differences. A meta-analysis of five replicated experiments would be quite different, in that the differences among messages within experiments provide a basis for estimating how much study-to-study variation to expect.

2. Methods for meta-analysis of replicated experiments are not yet well worked out, but the basic conceptual machinery required is available in Hedges and Olkin (1985, especially Chapter 9).

3. A simple alternative would have been to standardize the scores on each of the dependent measures, subjecting the standardized scores to mixed-model analysis of variance, as explained in Jackson (1991).

4. The relationship between d and r is quite simple. If n_1 is the size of the first treatment group and n_2 is the size of the second treatment group, then the following relationships hold between r, the correlation of the treatment variable with the dependent measure, and d, the standardized mean difference between the two treatment groups:

$$r = d/[d^2 + (n_1 + n_2 - 2)(n_1 + n_2)/(n_1 n_2)]^{1/2}$$
$$d = [(n_1 + n_2 - 2)(n_1 + n_2)/(n_1 n_2)]^{1/2} [r/(1 - r^2)^{1/2}]$$

When $n_1 = n_2$, these formulas simplify considerably, and the simplifications are reasonable approximations that may be used when the total N is known but not the individual group sizes.

5. The text assumes equal cell sizes, but if cell sizes are unequal, an approximation to unweighted means analysis can be worked out quite easily.

6. The differences arise not from divergent pictures of the phenomena but from computational choices such as the use of a bias correction applied to the effect-size measures and the use of a weighted mean effect size in place of the simple arithmetic mean of the effect sizes.

EIGHT

1. This distinction was suggested by Robert McPhee, in a round-table discussion of generalization at the November 1982 meetings of the Speech Communication Association.

REFERENCES

Allen, M., Hale, J., Mongeau, P., Berkowitz-Stafford, S., Stafford, S., Shanahan, W., Agee, P., Dillon, K., Jackson, R., & Ray, C. (1990). Testing a model of message sidedness: Three replications. *Communication Monographs*, *57*, 275–291.

Boster, F. J., & Mongeau, P. A. (1984). Fear arousing persuasive messages. In Bostrom, R. N. (Ed.), *Communication yearbook 8* (pp. 330–375). Beverly Hills, CA: Sage.

Burgoon, M., Hall, J., & Pfau, M. (1991). A test of the "messages-as-fixed-effect fallacy" argument: Empirical and theoretical implications of design choices. *Communication Quarterly*, *39*, 18–34.

Campbell, D. T., & Stanley, J. C. (1963). *Experimental and quasi-experimental designs for research*. Boston: Houghton-Mifflin.

Cappella, J. N. (1989). Re-making communication inquiry. In B. Dervin, L. Grossberg, B. J. O'Keefe, & E. Wartella (Eds.), *Rethinking communication, Vol. 1: Paradigm issues* (pp. 139–143). Newbury Park, CA: Sage.

Chow, S. L. (1987). Meta-analysis of pragmatic and theoretical research: A critique. *Journal of Psychology*, *121*, 259–271.

Clark, H. H. (1973). The language-as-fixed-effect fallacy: A critique of language statistics in psycholinguistics. *Journal of Verbal Learning and Verbal Behavior*, *12*, 335–359.

Clark, H. H. (1976). Reply to Wike and Church. *Journal of Verbal Learning and Verbal Behavior*, *15*, 257–261.

Clark, R. A., & Delia, J. G. (1977). Cognitive complexity, social perspective-taking and functional persuasive skills in second- to ninth-grade children. *Human Communication Research*, *3*, 128–134.

Cohen, J. (1976). Random means random. *Journal of Verbal Learning and Verbal Behavior*, *15*, 261–262.

Cohen, J. (1977). *Statistical power analysis for the behavioral sciences* (rev. ed.). New York: Academic.

Coleman, E. B. (1964). Generalizing to a language population. *Psychological Reports*, *14*, 219–226.

Cornfield, J. C., & Tukey, J. W. (1956). Average values of mean squares in factorials. *Annals of Mathematical Statistics*, *27*, 907–949.

Delia, J. G. (1976). Change of meaning processes in impression formation. *Communication Monographs*, *43*, 142–157.

Edgington, E. S. (1980). Randomization tests. New York: Marcel Dekker.

Efron, B. (1982). *The jackknife, the bootstrap and other resampling plans*. Philadelphia, PA: Society for Industrial and Applied Mathematics.

Ehninger, D. (1970). Argument as method. *Speech Monographs, 37,* 101–110.

Ellis, D. G. (1982). Language and speech communication. In M. Burgoon (Ed.), *Communication yearbook 6* (pp. 34–62). Beverly Hills, CA: Sage.

Finocchario, M. A. (1980). *Galileo and the art of reasoning: Rhetorical foundations of logic and scientific method*. Dordrecht: Reidel.

Forster, K. I., & Dickinson, R. G. (1976). More on the language-as-fixed-effect fallacy: Monte Carlo estimates of error rates for F_1, F_2, F', and min F'. *Journal of Verbal Learning and Verbal Behavior, 15,* 135–142.

Franklin, A. (1989). The epistemology of experiment. In D. Gooding, T. Pinch, & S. Schaffer (Eds.), *The uses of experiment: Studies in the natural sciences* (pp. 437–460). Cambridge, Eng.: Cambridge University Press.

Glass, G. V., & Hopkins, K. D. (1984). *Statistical methods in education and psychology* (2nd ed.). Englewood Cliffs, NJ: Prentice-Hall.

Glass, G. V., McGaw, B., & Smith, M. L. (1981). *Meta-analysis in social research*. Beverly Hills: Sage.

Gigerenzer, G., Swijtink, Z., Porter, T., Daston, L., Beatty, J., & Kruger, L. (1989). *The empire of chance: How probability changed science and everyday life*. Cambridge, Eng.: Cambridge University Press.

Hacking, I. (1965). *The logic of statistical inference*. Cambridge, MA: Basic.

Hedges, L. V., & Olkin, I. (1985). *Statistical methods for meta-analysis*. Orlando, FL: Academic.

Hewes, D. E. (1983). Confessions of a methodological Puritan: A response to Jackson and Jacobs. *Human Communication Research, 9,* 187–191.

Hopper, R. L., & Stucky, N. (1986, November). *"Message" research in the future*. Paper presented at the annual meetings of the Speech Communication Association, Chicago.

Hosman, L. (1987). The evaluational consequences of topic reciprocity and self-disclosure reciprocity. *Communication Monographs, 54,* 420–435.

Hunter, J. E., Hamilton, M. L., & Allen, M. (1989). The design and analysis of language experiments in communication. *Communication Monographs, 56,* 341–363.

Hunter, J. E., Schmidt, F. L., & Jackson, G. B. (1982). *Meta-analysis: Cumulating research findings across studies*. Beverly Hills, CA: Sage.

Jackson, S. (1986). Building a case for claims about discourse structure. In D. G. Ellis & W. A. Donohue (Eds.), *Contemporary issues in language and discourse processes* (pp. 129–147). Hillsdale, NJ: Erlbaum.

Jackson, S. (1989). Method as argument. In B. Gronbeck (Ed.), *Spheres of argument: Proceedings of the Sixth SCA/AFA Conference on Argumentation* (pp. 1–8). Annandale, VA: Speech Communication Association.

Jackson, S. (1991). Meta-analysis for primary and secondary data analysis: The super-experiment metaphor. *Communication Monographs, 58,* 449–462.

Jackson, S., & Backus, D. (1982). Are persuasive strategies systematically related to situational variables? *Central States Speech Journal, 33*, 469–479.

Jackson, S., & Brashers, D. (1990, June). *M = ? (Choosing a "message sample" size in communication experiments)*. Paper presented at the annual meetings of the International Communication Association, Dublin.

Jackson, S., & Jacobs, S. (1983). Generalizing about messages: Suggestions for the design and analysis of experiments. *Human Communication Research, 9*, 169–181.

Jackson, S., O'Keefe, D. J., & Jacobs, S. (1988). The search for reliable generalizations about messages: A comparison of research strategies. *Human Communication Research, 15*, 127–141.

Jackson, S., O'Keefe, D. J., Jacobs, S., & Brashers, D. (1989). Messages as replications: Toward a message-centered design strategy. *Communication Monographs, 56*, 364–384.

Janis, I. L., & Feshbach, S. (1953). Effects of fear-arousing communications. *Journal of Abnormal and Social Psychology, 48*, 78–92.

Kauffeld, F. (1989). Prima facie argumentative adequacy in the Federalist papers. In B. Gronbeck (Ed.), *Spheres of argument: Proceedings of the Sixth SCA/AFA Conference on Argumentation* (pp. 373–382). Annandale, VA: Speech Communication Association.

Kay, E. J., & Richter, M. L. (1977). The category confound: A design error. *Journal of Social Psychology, 103*, 57–63.

Keppel, G. (1976). Words as random variables. *Journal of Verbal Learning and Verbal Behavior, 15*, 263–265.

Keppel, G. (1982). *Design and analysis: A researcher's handbook* (2nd ed.). Englewood Cliffs, NJ: Prentice-Hall.

Keppel, G. (1991). *Design and analysis: A researcher's handbook* (3rd ed.). Englewood Cliffs, NJ: Prentice-Hall.

Kuhn, T. S. (1962). *The structure of scientific revolutions*. Chicago: University of Chicago Press.

Laudan, L. (1984). *Science and values*. Berkeley: University of California Press.

Lustig, M. W., & King, S. W. (1980). The effect of communication apprehension and situation on communication strategy choices. *Human Communication Research, 7*, 74–82.

Maxwell, S. E., & Bray, J. H. (1986). Robustness of the quasi F statistic to violations of sphericity. *Psychological Bulletin, 99*, 416–421.

McCloskey, D. M. (1985). *The rhetoric of economics*. Madison, WI: University of Wisconsin Press.

McLaughlin, M. L., Cody, M. J., & Robey, C. S. (1980). Situational influence on the selection of strategies to resist compliance-gaining attempts. *Human Communication Research, 7*, 14–36.

Miller, G., Boster, F., Roloff, M., & Seibold, D. (1977). Compliance-gaining message strategies: A typology and some findings concerning effects of situational differences. *Communication Monographs, 44*, 37–51.

Moerman, M. (1988). *Talking culture: Ethnography and conversation analysis.* Philadelphia, PA: University of Pennsylvania Press.

Morley, D. D. (1988). Meta-analytic techniques: When generalizing to message populations is not possible. *Human Communication Research, 15,* 112–126.

Nelson, J., McGill, A., & McCloskey, D. N. (1987) *The rhetoric of the human sciences.* Madison, WI: University of Wisconsin Press.

Nickles, T. R. (1989). Justification and experiment. In D. Gooding, T. Pinch, & S. Schaffer (Eds.), *The uses of experiment: Studies in the natural sciences* (pp. 299–333). Cambridge, Eng.: Cambridge University Press.

O'Keefe, B. J., & McCornack, S. A. (1987). Message design logic and message goal structure: Effects on perceptions of message quality in regulative communication situations. *Human Communication Research, 14,* 68–92.

O'Keefe, D. J. (1987, November). *Message description.* Paper presented at the annual meetings of the Speech Communication Association, Boston, MA.

O'Keefe, D. J. (1990). *Persuasion theory and research.* Newbury Park, CA: Sage.

Orne, M. T. (1969). Demand characteristics and the concept of quasi-controls. In R. Rosenthal & R. L. Rosnow (Eds.), *Artifact in behavioral research* (pp. 143–179). New York: Academic.

Polya, G. (1954). *Mathematics and plausible reasoning, Vol 1: Induction and analogy in mathematics.* Princeton, NJ: Princeton University Press.

Porter, T. M. (1986). *The rise of statistical thinking 1820–1900.* Princeton, NJ: Princeton University Press.

Rescher, N. (1976). *Plausible reasoning.* Amsterdam: van Gorcum.

Richter, M. L., & Seay, M. B. (1987). ANOVA designs with subjects and stimuli as random effects: Applications to prototype effects on recognition memory. *Journal of Personality and Social Psychology, 53,* 470–480.

Rogers, R. W., & Mewborn, C. R. (1976). Fear appeals and attitude change: Effects of a threat's noxiousness, probability of occurrence, and the efficacy of coping responses. *Journal of Personality and Social Psychology, 34,* 54–61.

Rosenthal, R. (1969). Interpersonal expectations: Effects of the experimenter's hypothesis. In R. Rosenthal & R. L. Rosnow (Eds.), *Artifact in behavioral research* (pp. 181–277). New York: Academic.

Rosenthal, R. (1976). *Experimenter effects in behavioral research* (enlarged ed.). New York: Irvington.

Santa, J. L., Miller, J. J., & Shaw, M. L. (1979). Using quasi *F* to prevent alpha inflation due to stimulus variation. *Psychological Bulletin, 86,* 37–46.

Schenkein, J. J. (Ed.). (1978). *Studies in the organization of conversational interaction.* New York: Academic.

Shimanoff, S. B. (1987). Types of emotional disclosures and request compliance between spouses. *Communication Monographs, 54,* 85–100.

Sillars, A. L. (1980). Attributions and communication in roommate conflicts. *Communication Monographs, 47,* 180–200.

Stigler, S. M. (1986). *The history of statistics: The measurement of uncertainty before 1900.* Cambridge, MA: Belknap.

Thomas, E. A. C., & Parpal, M. (1987). Liability as a function of plaintiff and defendant fault. *Journal of Personality and Social Psychology, 53,* 843857.

Toulmin, S. E. (1958). *The uses of argument.* Cambridge, Eng.: Cambridge University Press.

Vaughan, G. M., & Corballis, M. C. (1969). Beyond tests of significance: Estimating strength of effects in selected ANOVA designs. *Psychological Bulletin, 72,* 204–213.

Wickens, T. D., & Keppel, G. (1983). On the choice of design and of test statistic in the analysis of experiments with sampled materials. *Journal of Verbal Learning and Verbal Behavior, 22,* 296–309.

Wike, E. L., & Church, J. D. (1976). Comments on Clark's "The language-as-fixed-effect fallacy." *Journal of Verbal Learning and Verbal Behavior, 15,* 249–255.

Winer, B. J. (1971). *Statistical principles in experimental design* (2nd ed.). New York: McGraw-Hill.

INDEX